Culinary Taste
Consumer Behaviour in the International Restaurant Sector

Edited by **Donald Sloan**

Head of the Department of Hospitality,
Leisure and Tourism Management
Oxford Brookes University, UK

Routledge
Taylor & Francis Group

LONDON AND NEW YORK

First published 2004 by Butterworth-Heinemann

This edition published 2011 by Routledge
2 Park Square, Milton Park, Abingdon, Oxfordshire OX14 4RN
711 Third Avenue, New York, NY 10017

First issued in hardback 2016

Routledge is an imprint of the Taylor and Francis Group, an informa business

British Library Cataloguing in Publication Data
Sloan, Donald
    Culinary taste : consumer behaviour in the international restaurant sector
    1. Consumer behavior 2. Restaurant management
    I. Title
    658.8'342

Library of Congress Cataloging-in-Publication Data
Culinary taste : consumer behaviour in the international restaurant sector /
edited by Donald Sloan. – 1st ed.
        p. cm.
    Includes index.
    ISBN 0-7506-5767-7
        1. Gastronomy. 2. Food habits. I. Sloan, Donald.

TX631.C85 2003
641'.01'3–dc22   2003049439

ISBN 13: 978-1-138-15159-8 (hbk)
ISBN 13: 978-0-7506-5767-9 (pbk)

Contents

Hospitality, Leisure & Tourism Series

Acknowledgements

The challenging task of editing this text has been considerably eased by the willing and enthusiastic involvement of a range of colleagues and friends. I am extremely grateful, of course, to those who have contributed chapters. It is my pleasure to acknowledge the role of Professor Conrad Lashley, Series Editor, who offered much welcome support when I first put forward a proposal for this work. Sally North and Holly Bennett of Butterworth-Heinemann have managed the production process in a patient and professional manner. A crucial role has been played by Kathryn Black, who undertook the considerable task of formatting the text in her characteristically efficient and good-humoured style.

My thanks go to Julia Sibley and Margaret Georgiou of the Savoy Educational Trust for the generous support that they continue to provide, which facilitates gastronomic research amongst staff at Oxford Brooks University. Finally, I would like to thank those who in recent years have been involved in teaching gastronomy at Oxford Brookes University, whether as seminar leaders or as guest speakers, and who have been responsible for stimulating interest in this fascinating subject among our students. In this respect my thanks go to Nina Becket, Raymond Blanc, David Fouillé, Prue Leith, Peter McGunnigle, Candy Morley, Diane Seymour and Rick Stein.

Donald Sloan
Oxford, 2003

Contributors

David Bell is Head of Media, Journalism and Cultural Studies at Staffordshire University. He teaches cultural studies, and his research interests include food consumption, cybercultures, cultural policy, urban and rural cultures and sexual politics.

Maureen Brookes is Undergraduate Programme Director and a Senior Lecturer in Marketing in the Department of Hospitality, Leisure and Tourism at Oxford Brookes University. As a graduate of Canada's University of Guelph, she held a variety of management positions with international hotel groups before coming to England as Owner/Director of a hotel in the Cotswolds. Her research and publications have focused on the centric orientation of international hotel groups, international marketing standardization, interdisciplinary research and student satisfaction. She is currently investigating the management of international hotel groups as 'diverse affiliations' for a PhD degree.

Dr Marion Demossier is Senior Lecturer in French and European Studies at the University of Bath. She is the author of various works on wine producers and wine consumers in France and has published on culture, heritage and identity in France and Europe. Her teaching is mainly in French and European Politics and Society. Her first monograph *Hommes*

Hospitality, Leisure & Tourism Series

et Vins, une anthropologie du vignoble bourguignon (1999, Editions Universitaires de Dijon) won the Prix Lucien Perriaux. She is the Treasurer for ICAF Europe (International Commission for the Anthropology of Food) and is currently writing a book entitled *An Anthropology of Wine Culture and Consumption in France*.

Joanne Finkelstein trained as a sociologist at the University of Illinois, Urbana, USA. Her research interests are in global consumer trends. She is the author of four books, which explore various aspects of consumption, fashion and aesthetics. These are: *Slaves of Chic* (Minerva); *The Fashioned Self* (Polity); *Dining Out* (Polity); and *After a Fashion* (NYU). A further book on *Spin and the Art of Modern Manners* will be available in 2004. She is Professor of Sociology at the University of Sydney, Australia, and the Director of Postgraduate Research in the Faculty of Arts. She teaches in cultural theory.

David Fouillé lectures in gastronomy at the International Hotel Management Institute and International Tourism Institute, Luzern, Switzerland. Previously he was an Associate Lecturer in the Department of Hospitality, Leisure and Tourism Management at Oxford Brookes University and he worked for Petit Blanc Restaurants in both Oxford and Birmingham. His interest in gastronomy and his love of wine emerged during his formative years in Saumur, in the Loire Valley, and were further developed while undertaking his German hotel apprenticeship and his Bachelor's degree at Oxford Brookes University.

Professor Conrad Lashley is Head of the Centre for Leisure Retailing at Nottingham Business School. He is also Series Editor for Butterworth-Heinemann's *Hospitality, Leisure and Tourism Series*. He has author, co-authored or edited 16 books and published reports including *In Search of Hospitality: Theoretical Perspectives and Debates*, which attempts to understand hospitality through social science perspectives. His research interests focus on issues related to the emotional dimensions of hospitality from management, frontline employee and guest's points of view.

Prue Leith sold her restaurant, catering company and cookery school in 1995 when she also stopped writing cookbooks. Since then she has written three novels (two about restaurants and catering) and is currently on the Boards of Whitbread and Woolworth. She is Chair of the British Food Trust, Ashridge Management College and Forum for the Future.

Dr Alison Morrison is Reader in Hospitality Management and Director of Research within the Scottish Hotel School, University of Strathclyde. She has attained a BA Hotel and Catering Management from the University of Strathclyde, an MSc in Entrepreneurship from Stirling University and a PhD from the University of Strathclyde with the thesis titled *Small Firm Strategic Alliances: The UK Hotel Industry*. Alison has edited and authored five textbooks in the areas of marketing, hospitality, entrepreneurship and franchising and has published widely in generic business and specialist hospitality and tourism academic journals.

Sandie Randall is Head of Hospitality, Tourism and Leisure at Queen Margaret University College, Edinburgh. Her recent research interests and publications have been concerned with the cultural aspects of food and hospitality, the production and consumption of media representations of food and the use of semiotics as an analytical research tool.

Diane Seymour is a sociologist teaching and researching in the Department of Hospitality, Leisure and Tourism Management at Oxford Brookes University. Her teaching includes undergraduate modules on work organization, gastronomy and leisure and postgraduate work on intercultural diversity. She has previously researched and published on the sociology of food, emotional labour and international management competence. Her current research interests remain broadly in these three areas though her passion for France and the French language is leading her to focus more on developing her work in the sociology of food.

Donald Sloan is Head of the Department of Hospitality, Leisure and Tourism Management at Oxford Brookes University.

He teaches gastronomy, and his current research interests relate to influences on culinary taste and associated consumer behaviour. He was the first recipient of the Martin Radcliffe Fellowship in Gastronomy, which is funded by the Savoy Educational Trust.

Dr Roy C. Wood is Principal and Managing Director of the International Hotel Management Institute and International Tourism Institute, Luzern, Switzerland. Prior to this, he was Professor of Hospitality Management at the University of Strathclyde, UK from 1996 to 2003. He is the author, co-author or editor of some 13 books and over 60 papers in referred journals. He has published extensively on the sociology of food and eating as well as on human resource issues in hospitality and tourism. His current research interests are in the field of argumentation analysis and rhetoric in organizations and the relationships between creativity and innovation in hospitality product development.

Foreword

Prue Leith

This book is really welcome, and long overdue. Since I started my career as a cook, and still think of myself first and foremost as a cook, it is not surprising that I should think that gastronomy matters. But for many people, including those in the hospitality profession, it does not seem to, other than as a means of bettering the bottomline. Food is seen as a product – which of course it is. But food is much more than that.

Our attitudes to it are crucial and are governed by factors such as class, race, religion, age, upbringing, health and our social environment. Why is it that Inuit people can live on a high-protein, blubber-laden diet and be healthy? Why is it that young Western women, surrounded by every opportunity to eat healthily, are so prone to anorexia and bulimia?

Trends in the hospitality industry are fascinating. In the 40 years I have been in the business I have seen astonishing changes. The fifties in Britain, still under the shadow of rationing and wartime make-do-and-mend of the previous decade, gradually gave way to cautious acceptance of 'foreign food' in the sixties. Garlic became something one ate for pleasure, rather than swallowed in capsules to purify the blood. Olive oil moved from an earache soother to the salad bowl. The end of the seventies and the excessive eighties saw the beginning of *nouvelle cuisine*, with its 'little bit of nothing on a big white plate' – to my mind a direct reflection of the jaded palate of our over-worked and over-paid boom-time customers: no one who has had a breakfast meeting and a lunch meeting, and a lot of champagne at drinks time, wants a lot of food. But they were prepared to pay a lot for a very little of it. Food had become a status symbol, with little to do with nutrition. The eighties boom ended in bust of course, and guess what? – our customers no longer wanted elaborate concoctions: they wanted comfort food, and lots of it, in bowls.

But why should we care about any of this? Well, first of all because it is riveting stuff. And then because food is pretty important. Not just because it keeps us alive, but because it defines us, socially and economically. We ought, I think to know why we eat certain things. Do children eat MacDonalds burgers because they like them? Because their parents do? Because their friends do? Because they can afford them? Because the advertisements and commercials persuade them to? If you are going to market a fast food product, would not that be interesting to know?

Do most customers buy the second-cheapest wine because they are frightened of the wine waiter, because they know the name, because they like the wine, because they don't want to be ostentatious? Do some customers always buy the best because they are connoisseurs? Or show-offs, or trying to impress their guests. Or are they frightened of the wine waiter?

The sociology of food preferences is totally fascinating.

In the hospitality business we all know that if we are to succeed we need to understand our customers. Our customers eat (probably) food three times a day. It has got to pay to understand where they are coming from, even if they do not quite know themselves. To know what trends are around the corner, what influences will change our customers' perceptions.

I thoroughly recommend this book. The contributions are varied and fascinating and will, I am sure, engage you further in that most wonderful of subjects – food.

Prue Leith
2003

Introduction

Donald Sloan

The broad purpose of this text is to examine the construction of culinary taste, and associated consumer behaviour, as displayed in the international restaurant sector. It is often noted that sociological commentary on food and eating is dominated by studies relating to domestic settings. The recent emergence of more literature which examines aspects of dining out has begun to redress this imbalance (see e.g. Finkelstein, 1989; Warde, 1997; Gronow, 1997; Beardsworth and Keil, 1997; Warde and Martens, 2000; Wood, 2000). This text adds to this growing body of knowledge.

Discussions about the construction of taste, and culinary taste in particular, are undoubtedly fascinating in their own right. However, it is important not to overlook the potential practical benefits of extending our knowledge in this area. Business texts often assert the importance of restaurateurs meeting customer needs and wants, yet few tackle the complex question of what actually influences customer choices. Where this question is addressed it is often done so in a rather formulaic manner which encompasses consideration of issues such as price versus quality.

The first two chapters provide an introduction to alternative theoretical perspectives on the construction of culinary taste. Subsequent chapters, the content of which is more explicitly applied to consumer behaviour in the international restaurant sector, examine specific aspects of influence on culinary taste.

The initial discussion, which centres on the contribution of French sociologist Pierre Bourdieu, examines the proposal that our taste is socially constructed; specifically the extent to which our position in the socio-economic class hierarchy predisposes us towards adopting and displaying particular forms of culinary taste. The subtleties of Bourdieu's arguments are addressed, in areas such as the role of taste as a signifier of class distinction (including of distinction between intra-class fractions); the use of taste acquisition by the socially aspirant; the achievement of cultural legitimacy through expressions of taste; and the role that taste plays within struggles for class domination.

Chapter 2 examines the postmodern perspective. Sociologists such as Bauman and Beck have argued that rigid class hierarchies, which emerged to support modernist industrial systems, are no longer in place, and the proposition that taste is influenced by adherence to class conventions is, therefore, redundant. Instead, what has supposedly emerged is an individualized society in which self-identities, and their expression through consumer behaviour, are constructed on a personal rather than collective basis. Chapter 2 goes on to examine whether in our aestheticized, consumerist society, new forms of social alliance are emerging which are signified by adherence to various forms of lifestyle. In addition, is our growing preoccupation with lifestyle characteristic of a democratized society in which more traditional forms of social distinction are becoming less visible?

Lifestyles, and their influence on culinary taste within cosmopolitan urban settings, are analysed by David Bell in *Taste and space: eating out in the city today*. Bell argues that in our postindustrial cities, which have now adopted symbolic economies, dining out is representative of wider cultural characteristics. Cultural status marking is played out through restaurant dining and the acquisition of cultural capital results from association with particular restaurants and restaurant sectors. While opportunities for the development of cultural capital and a credible self-identity might seem appealing, Bell notes that the proliferation of choice in the restaurant market can be a source of anxiety and confusion. In addition, while restaurateurs can undoubtedly benefit from understanding current consumer preferences, they have to remember that fashions are fickle. Bell highlights this point in relation to ethnic cuisines, the perceived authenticity and fashionability of which can diminish as they become progressively more accessible.

In *Chic cuisine: the impact of fashion on food*, Joanne Finkelstein explores the proposal that dining out in the postmodern era is as much to do with fashion as it is to do with culinary appreciation. Beginning with a deconstruction of the meanings of artworks, which have been constructed using food products, Finkelstein establishes that food can have significance beyond that which is obvious. She asserts that much about contemporary life can be understood through observation of dining practices, particularly the widespread desire to display fashionability and sophistication.

Roy C. Wood's *The shock of the new: a sociology of nouvelle cuisine*, was originally published back in 1991 in the *Journal of Consumer Studies and Home Economics*. Its inclusion in this text seemed highly appropriate, not least because Wood examines whether the emergence of *nouvelle cuisine* represented a rebellion against Escoffierian cuisine being regarded as the epitome of good taste. To this end, Wood undertakes a cultural, rather than a culinary, analysis of nouvelle cuisine. He identifies associations with individuality; creativity; superiority; and distinction, which signify the extent to which nouvelle cuisine had an impact on perceptions of tastefulness.

In *Contemporary lifestyles: the case of wine*, Marion Demossier begins by identifying what has led to greater accessibility, variety and consumer knowledge in the wine market. She goes on to discuss what the nature of wine consumption reveals about our cultural environment. For example, to what extent does wine knowledge and an ability to master the rituals of wine consumption signify the possession of cultural capital? Conversely, is the distinction that is the prize for wine consumers heightened through the intimidation that the inexperienced might suffer?

Maureen Brookes, in *Shaping culinary taste: the influence of commercial operators*, investigates whether restaurants can actually shape culinary taste, or whether they simply respond to culinary taste. Brookes begins by identifying the impact of changing demographics and work patterns on consumer preferences. This

Hospitality, Leisure & Tourism Series

provides the context in which to examine how consumers construct their preferences. Brookes proposes that the role of the meal in the process is declining as more intangible issues, such as the symbolic meaning we attach to branded restaurant chains, come to the fore.

In Roy C. Wood's second contribution, *Gender and culinary taste* he notes that despite the existence of popular assumptions regarding women's culinary taste there is actually little empirical evidence in this area. Even when the issue is raised in relation to domestic dining, it tends to be entangled within commentary on social class. However, drawing on the commentary on domestic dining, Wood provides convincing speculation about the influence of gender on culinary taste. In particular, he discusses the consequences of dominant patriarchal systems on areas such as food choice, food production and menu construction.

David Fouille, in *Developing a taste for health*, highlights the extent to which dietary awareness and respect for high quality ingredients are positive trends, which appear to have been encouraged recently by various high profile food-related crises. He presents the relatively optimistic view that the maintenance of such trends requires greater culinary awareness, which might signify a long-term commitment to quality among restaurant customers.

Finally, Conrad Lashley, Alison Morrison and Sandie Randall provide a fascinating insight into influences on contemporary culinary taste through a study of the dining experiences of a group of students. Using semiotic analysis, Lashley et al. reveal the meanings hidden within the students' narratives about their most memorable meals. Their analysis displays the powerful cultural and social associations which exist within the students' commentary and, to an extent, the subordinate role of food within the meal experience.

Readers are likely to identify a common theme that runs through each of the chapters. In essence, it should be clear that our culinary taste, and our associated consumer behaviour, are greatly influenced by the wider cultural context in which we operate. All contributors to this text are in agreement that culinary taste is socially constructed. However, what this text also reveals is that the nature of social influence is highly complex.

Bibliography

Beardsworth, A. and Keil, T. (1997). *Sociology on the Menu.* London: Routledge.

Gronow, J. (1997). *The Sociology of Taste.* London: Routledge.

Finkelstein, J. (1989). *Dining Out.* Cambridge: Polity Press.

Warde, A. (1997). *Consumption, Food and Taste.* London: Sage Publications.

Warde, A. and Martens, L. (2000). *Eating Out: Social Differentiation, Consumption and Pleasure.* Cambridge: Cambridge University Press.

Wood, R.C. (Ed.) (2000). *Strategic Questions in Food and Beverage Management.* Oxford: Butterworth-Heinemann.

The social construction of taste

Diane Seymour

This chapter examines the argument that taste is socially constructed and that the food tastes we have and the choices we make about what to eat are determined by social factors. For example, although man is omnivorous, the cultural rules governing what is defined as good to eat, the way it is prepared, cooked or not cooked, served and eaten vary between cultures in often quite dramatic ways (Scholliers, 2001), and these definitions change through time (Elias, 1978). Thus it is possible to conceive of the construction of taste as occurring within a framework of rules at different levels; the level of culture generally, including cultural rules expressed in food ways or cuisine, filtered through other layers such as region, religion, class, caste, gender, family and so on. This explains how individual tastes can be different within a family; choices are indeed different but they are made within a relatively narrow framework of possibilities provided by position in the social structure. There are in addition the influences of medical advice, the state and of food suppliers. However, this chapter focuses on the arguments concerning the influence of social class in particular.

Bourdieu and the social construction of taste

Any discussion of the social construction of taste must begin with the seminal work of the French sociologist, Pierre Bourdieu. Bourdieu was not just interested in cultural tastes but also in the way in which taste arises out of and is employed in struggles for social recognition and status. In 1979 he published 'Distinction: a social critique of the judgement of taste', a work which drew together his thinking across a range of disciplines and which explores the lifestyles of France's class structure (Bourdieu, 1984). Supported by an analysis of statistical data already in the public domain, he argued that our taste, and indeed all our consumption behaviour, is an expression of social class. Different social classes can be identified by the way in which they express their tastes in music, art, clothes, home decoration and of course the food they eat. However, his analysis of class does not depend on simple economic or materialist criteria. Nor does he argue that the construction of taste is a simple outcome of the deterministic processes of occupation or income: this is what makes his ideas on the social construction of taste so interesting and powerful.

Habitus

The concept of habitus is the link between the objective and the subjective components of class, that is, class as determined by largely economic factors, and class as a set of practices, dispositions and feelings. Habitus refers to the everyday, the situations, actions, practices and choices which tend to go with a particular walk of life and an individual's position in the social world (this includes, e.g. gender and race as well as class). Habitus therefore, can be seen as including a set of *dispositions*, tendencies to do some things rather than others and to do them in particular ways rather than in other ways. Habitus does not, therefore *determine* our practices, but it does make it more likely that we will adopt certain practices rather than others. The link with objective class position comes through a consideration of how habitus is acquired. To suggest that it is learned implies a self-consciousness that is absent in Bourdieu's conception. Here we need to draw on the concept of socialization to capture the way in which, although habitus is learned, this learning is acquired in an unselfconscious way simply by being immersed in a particular social milieu. The dispositions acquired through habitus are the ways of doing things that those sharing a particular social position think of as natural and obvious, common sense, and taken for granted. These dispositions do not prevent us from behaving in other ways, that is, they do not proscribe what we can or cannot do through a set of rules, but the patterns of behaviours common to a particular habitus become inculcated in our sense of who and what we are. So habitus *disposes* individuals to make certain choices. While we do not *choose* practices as free individuals, neither are we forced or impelled into them; rather we behave in ways which seem obvious and reasonable given our social milieu. Thus habitus *could* be overridden by other considerations in certain circumstances; for example, rational calculation where an individual realizes that the way he or she is disposed to behave in a particular context is not the best response to that context (Bourdieu, 1979, p. 122). However, since habitus is embedded in class position, choices and tastes are a matter of class rather than of individual personality, or in other words our tastes are socially rather than individually constructed. Habitus and lifestyle on the one hand, and class position on the other, set limits on one another which, while not excluding the caviar eating road digger, make such a choice less likely. The tendency is that individuals sharing a particular habitus (and therefore class position) will react in similar ways, make similar choices and share similar judgements of tastes.

Habitus and social class

This brings us to a consideration of the class-based source of habitus. For Bourdieu, class position is not based crudely on the possession or non-possession of the means of production as in Marxist materialistic conceptions of class. He draws on the work of Weber, which allows him to identify different classes and fractions of classes in a hierarchical schema rather than to see class in terms of two classes in opposition to one another, although he retains the notion of struggle between the classes (to be considered further later). Bourdieu sees class as determined by the possession of differing amounts of different forms of capital. In simple economic terms, capital is what results from production, and in turn it goes towards feeding more production. For example, a restaurant is a form of economic capital. Once built, it is used to make other things (meals). The raw materials used and the money to buy them with are also forms of capital. Capital thus comes from production and in turn feeds more production; capital reproduces production. However, Bourdieu, in contrast to Marx, who only considered economic capital, extends the idea of capital to other aspects of the social, which he argues are themselves social products which are circulated and which can be used to produce further capital. Of these, cultural capital and symbolic capital are the most significant for our purposes, and are discussed further below.[1]

Non-economic forms of capital

So, then, economic capital is to do with products of the economy (goods and money). Cultural capital is to do with the circulation of cultural products and the reproduction of cultural relations. Cultural capital comes from possessing the kind of knowledge and familiarity with cultural products which enable a person to know how they work, what to say about them and how to appreciate and evaluate them. In essence, how to consume them. Cultural capital is acquired through immersion in habitus; it can be accumulated during a lifetime and passed on from generation to generation in just the same way as economic capital. Cultural capital may come from the actual possession of certain culturally valued artefacts such as paintings. It may derive from activities such as going to the opera or from appreciating fine wine, or from knowledge about cultural products.

Bourdieu distinguishes between *legitimate*, *middlebrow* and *working class* culture and identifies the tastes associated with each of these categories, and for class fractions within them. While it is possible to acquire legitimate cultural capital (i.e. the definitions and judgements of taste possessed by the dominant

classes) through individual effort or education, such expressions of learned tastes do not have the same status and social
standing as tastes which appear to be natural or innate.

> The myth of an innate taste ... is just one of the expres-
> sions of the recurrent illusion of a cultivated nature pre-
> dating any education. (Bourdieu et al., 1991, p. 109)

Thus to be cultivated, to be a master in the judgement of taste,
an appreciation of high culture must appear to be innate:

> Culture is only achieved by denying itself as such,
> namely as artificial and artificially acquired. (Bourdieu
> et al., 1991, p. 110)

Cultivated individuals experience their own distinction as
taken for granted and natural, as a mark of their social value. It
follows then that the working classes must lack the necessary
nature for a proper enjoyment of cultural products, and that this
explains their infrequent attendance at museums and galleries,
their consumption of heavy food and so on. To grow up in a
habitus which inculcates cultural capital is clearly an advantage
in other spheres. For example, Bourdieu argued that the cultural capital possessed by the dominant classes enabled them to
acquire educational capital much more easily than the lower
classes. The disposition to succeed in the educational system
and the familiarity with the codes and symbols of education, all
part of the habitus of the dominant classes, (Wilkes, 1990) leads
to the perpetuation of privilege, as educational capital can then
be converted into economic capital in the form of well paid jobs.

Symbolic capital is a form of cultural capital which refers to
the sphere of signs. All aspects of social behaviour carry the
potential to operate as a sign, or symbol, of an individual's
position. For example, the type of car an individual drives,
where he or she shops, what they wear, all these things carry
messages. However, the way in which the messages or signs
are interpreted may vary depending on the relative positions
of the bearer and the observer:

> Each lifestyle can only really be construed in relation to
> the other, which is its subjective and objective negation,

so that the meaning of behaviour is totally reversed depending on which point of view is adopted. (Bourdieu, 1984, p. 193)

Thus, what is valuable symbolic capital in one group is not necessarily worth much in another once these practices are removed from the particular habitus which gives them value. In this way, articles, behaviours and bodily gestures which signify membership of a particular class or class fraction may earn disapproval from members of a different habitus. Various forms of cultural capital compete to assert their own value, and the status of those who hold them. In this struggle, it is the cultural forms and symbols belonging to the most powerful social groups which are able to assert their definition as *legitimate* culture. So the signs and symbols used by the dominant classes to act as markers for their superior position acquire cultural legitimacy because of this very association with a superior habitus. Further, they present themselves not as arbitrary judgements of taste but as natural, and it is the culture of these dominant groups which define all others in their own terms, seeing the culture of subordinate groups as tasteless.

Different forms of capital can be exchanged for other forms of capital. Economic capital can be invested in cultural or symbolic capital and cultural capital can be converted into economic capital. The possession of varying amounts of different forms of capital produces and maintains class distinctions and fractions within classes. For example although in contemporary societies economic capital is the dominant form of capital which supports the broad class categories of upper class, middle class and working class, within these broad categories there are fractions distinguished by their possession or non-possession of cultural and symbolic capital. Bourdieu distinguishes, for example, within the upper classes, the dominant fraction of the dominant class (a fraction which possess high amounts of economic capital but relatively lower amounts of cultural capital) and the dominated fraction of the dominant class (a fraction which possesses high amounts of cultural capital but relatively less economic capital). These class fractions produce different habituses, and distinguish themselves by their different tastes. The appropriation of cultural practices by the dominant classes enables them to have a sense of distinction deriving from their habitus of legitimately established domination and the power to define and establish the boundaries of taste. The middle classes are characterized by what Bourdieu calls 'cultural good-will' (Bourdieu, 1979, p. 370); middle class habitus assumes the tone of conformity with the tastes of the dominant class to whose position they aspire, and which enables them to distinguish themselves from the working class. The expression of taste for this class will therefore ape (as far as economic and cultural capital will allow) the taste of the class above and will be characterized by a respect for culture, over-conventionality and over-conformity. However, the bourgeois sense of ease and belonging is absent for the middle classes whose acquisition of cultural practices is only acquired through effort and application. In terms of eating out for example, upwardly mobile middle class groups seeking to copy the restaurant choices or restaurant behaviours of the upper classes might not feel altogether at ease, might feel out of their depth or might struggle to enjoy the food. In addition, of course, their relative lack of economic capital would mean that the cost of this sort of meal could only be justified for a special occasion, adding to the sense of unease. For the working classes taste is the choice of the necessary; a working class habitus is established out of the necessity for the material conditions of existence which values and makes a virtue of the plain, the unpretentious, the useful, the convenient and the practical. For example, eating out is likely to be relatively less frequent and may be in the context of a pub restaurant, a supermarket restaurant or workplace canteen (Warde and Martens, 2000).

Strategies of distinction

The fiercest struggles for cultural legitimacy are conducted between the social groups which border one another. In this way, cultural capital contests the dominance of economic capital through strategies of *distinction*. These strategies focus on issues of taste. Tastes make distinctions between things and practices and endow those who adopt them with distinction. In addition tastes, which are in fact socially constructed, are identified through apparently individual attributes (e.g. the ability to appreciate quality). It follows then, that the working classes do not take part in these struggles but they nevertheless play a role for the classes above them. These classes, especially the middle classes, seek to demonstrate through their practices and judgements of taste a distance from the vulgarity and tastelessness (as defined by the dominant classes) of the working classes.

High cultural capital is relatively rare, and those who possess it battle to protect its exclusivity. After all, if a group's distinction is challenged by more and more people acquiring the objects, skills or knowledge peculiar to it, then its position is threatened. When the class fraction possessing high cultural capital is threatened in this way, for example, by wider educational opportunities, a drop in price of previously expensive goods, etc. then it changes its signifying objects and tastes in order to retain the distinguishing distance from other class fractions. Thus the signs and symbols which signify distinction and the practices which demonstrate taste, are open to constant change and redefinition. This struggle to adopt new practices to act as markers of distinction could be used to explain, for example, the changing patronage of different restaurants. As social groups lower in the hierarchy struggle to obtain a greater amount of economic and cultural capital and begin to adopt the tastes of the groups above them, these higher social groups must find new practices and tastes in order to preserve their distinction and their claim to superiority. Thus contrary to some accounts of Bourdieu's work (e.g. Warde, 1997) consumption behaviour and taste are not simply *expressions* of class position but are part of the struggle for dominance and legitimacy between the social classes and fractions of classes.

The construction of culinary taste

Let us now turn to how Bourdieu uses this theoretical framework to explain the ways in which culinary taste is socially constructed through habitus. He observes, first, that a simple reading of the statistics of the consumption of different foods leads commentators to:

See a simple effect of income in the fact that, as one rises in the social hierarchy, the proportion of income spent on

> food diminishes, or that, within the food budget, the pro-
> portion spent on heavy, fatty, fattening foods, which are
> also cheap … declines. (Bourdieu, 1984, p. 177).

However, as he goes on to point out, this simple explanation cannot account for differences in tastes and consumption between social groups who share similar incomes but have very different food consumption patterns. The broad opposition corresponding to income masks more subtle oppositions within the classes. Within the dominant and middle classes in particular, Bourdieu distinguishes differences between the fractions relatively richer in cultural capital and those relatively richer in economic capital. These differences in the volume and structure of global capital give rise to different habituses and lifestyles within the broad class groupings which are expressed in different tastes in food consumption (see Table 1.1). However, the real principle governing these differences in tastes in food is the opposition between the 'tastes of luxury (or freedom) and the tastes of necessity' (Bourdieu, 1979, p. 198). Tastes are shaped by the material conditions of existence; the tastes of luxury are the tastes of individuals born into a habitus that is defined by distance from necessity who possess therefore the freedoms stemming from possession of capital. The tastes of necessity derive from the necessity of producing labour power at the lowest cost; hence the preference for heavy, filling foods among the working classes. For Bourdieu, then, the very idea of taste, since it presupposes freedom of choice, is a bourgeois notion. However, the question of taste is more complex than this. He goes on to argue that it would be a mistake to assume that food tastes and practices are a direct product of economic necessity. Rather, the taste of necessity (which derives from the volume of economic capital) becomes the basis of a habitus and lifestyle that makes a virtue of necessity so that individuals acquire 'a taste for what they are anyway condemned to' (Bourdieu, 1979, p. 199).

Bourdieu goes on to analyse patterns of spending on what he calls three styles of distinction[2] in which the basic opposition between the tastes of luxury and the tastes of necessity is expressed through consumption patterns in different ways by different class fractions within the dominant class. Each of these different habituses has a different way of asserting its

Type of capital possessed and characteristic tastes	Relatively high consumption	Relatively low consumption
Employers: high economic but relatively lower cultural capital *Taste for:* food rich in cost and calories – heavy, meals have many courses, with dishes containing rare and expensive ingredients *Meal preparation:* time consuming, complicated dishes *Opposition with subordinate groups* expressed in terms of lack of economic restraints rather than a change in tastes	Cakes and pastries, wine and aperitifs, meat preserves (e.g. foie gras), game	Fresh meat, fruit and vegetables, restaurant and canteen meals
Teachers: high cultural but lower economic capital *Taste for:* ascetic consumption and originality, exotic cuisine, (e.g. ethnic restaurants/culinary populism) ('traditional' peasant dishes) *Meal preparation:* simple, easily and quickly prepared dishes, making use of pre-prepared ingredients *Opposition expressed by* the pursuit of originality at least cost and disapproval of the rich and heavy food habits of the upper and lower classes	Bread, milk products, sugar, fruit preserves, non-alcoholic drinks, canteen meals, ethnic restaurant meals	Wine and spirits, meat especially expensive cuts, fresh fruit and vegetables, coffee, tea
Professionals: medium economic, medium cultural capital *Taste for:* light, refined, delicate food, traditional cuisine, rich in expensive/ rare products *Meal preparation:* characterized by low calorie, low fat light food, time saving dishes *Opposition with subordinate groups* expressed by distinctions in taste: economic constraints disappear but are replaced by social proscriptions forbidding coarseness and fatness, admiration for slim	Meat especially expensive cuts (e.g. lamb, veal), fresh fruit and vegetables, fish, shellfish, aperitifs, restaurant meals	Meat preserves, cakes and pastries, sugar, non-alcoholic drinks, canteen meals

Adapted from Bourdieu (1979, p. 206).

Table 1.1 Food tastes and food consumption patterns of the upper class fractions

Type of capital possessed and characteristic tastes	Relatively high consumption	Relatively low consumption
Low economic and cultural capital *Taste for:* cheap, high calorie, high fat, heavy cuisine (e.g. nourishing casseroles) *Meal preparation:* cooked dishes needed high time investment (e.g. cassoulet and ouillette) *Opposition with dominant classes* expressed by values about good living: to eat well, drink well, enjoy generous open hospitality	Bread, cooked meats, milk, cheese, cheap cuts of meat especially pork	Fresh fruit and vegetables, restaurant and canteen meals, fish, shellfish

Adapted from Bourdieu (1979, pp. 206–209).

Table 1.2 Food tastes and food consumption patterns of the working classes

distance from the tastes of necessity of the working classes. Taking food as the example, Bourdieu distinguishes marked differences between the industrial and commercial employers on the one hand and the teachers and professionals on the other in the way they express their tastes in their spending patterns (see Table 1.1). These differences express the ways in which these class fractions distinguish themselves from the tastes of necessity which characterize the tastes of the working class (see Table 1.2).

This enables Bourdieu to construct a map of food space and to predict the kinds of tastes different fractions will have, depending on the particular combinations of cultural and economic capital (see Table 1.3). Those class fractions high in economic capital and lower in cultural capital tend to prefer relatively high amounts of rich, strong, fatty, salty food, whereas those high in cultural capital and lower in economic capital prefer healthy, natural, exotic foods. In contrast, the taste of those low in both forms of capital is for cheap, salty, fatty, strong, simmered and nourishing foods. The taste for particular dishes is inextricably linked to the lifestyles of a particular habitus since it is associated with a particular division of domestic labour and domestic economy. A taste for elaborate

Hospitality, Leisure & Tourism Series

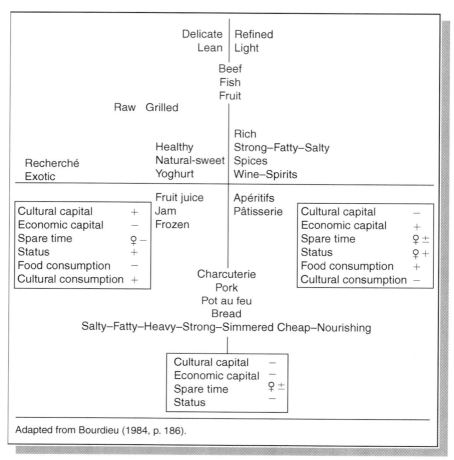

Table 1.3 The food space map

casserole dishes, which demand considerable investment of time is linked to a traditional conception of a woman's role (or the availability of domestic servants). This produces a strong opposition between the working classes and the dominated fractions of the dominant classes in which women are likely to pursue careers. In these latter class fractions, women spend their time on child care and the transmission of cultural capital rather than on traditional domestic labour, which combined with the value of healthy ascetic refined living suggests light low calorie quickly prepared dishes. These differences are reflected too in different ways of serving and consuming food. Bourdieu discerns an opposition between the free and easy working class meal (characterized by elastic dishes which do not require cutting and counting and thus give an impression of abundance, second helpings for men, without strict sequencing of the meal), and the concern for form which characterizes the bourgeois meal. These differences in the approach to the meal reflect the different habitus of the dominant and working classes. The habitus of the dominant classes represents the bourgeois relation to the social world, which is one of order, restraint, propriety and aesthetics. Through the forms imposed on the appetite, food tastes and associated behavioural traits, become elements in the art of living and the expression of refinement, in opposition to and rejection of the animal nature and material vulgarity of primary needs and the classes who indulge these needs without restraint.

Bourdieu explores the different relationships to the social world expressed by habitus through a detailed analysis of attitudes towards entertaining derived from surveys conducted in 1978. Here the opposition is between substance (the content of the meal, informality, the fun of the social occasion) emphasized in the working class habitus, and form (etiquette, manners, table décor, formality of dress and behaviour) characteristic of the bourgeois habitus. It is here, he argues, that these two antagonistic world views are thrown into sharpest relief; antagonistic because they each represent opposite conceptions of human excellence deriving from opposing relationships to the material conditions of existence. On the one hand, it is substance which matters, not only filling but 'real'; the small café where 'you get an honest square meal and "are not paying for the wallpaper" ' (Bourdieu, 1984, p. 199). On the other it is form, where expressions of distinction and power take precedence; a concern for symbolism and aesthetic art of living, a commitment to stylization and a preference for quality over quantity.

A final point needs to be made about the nature of class reproduction. We have seen that Bourdieu argued that classes and class fractions reproduce themselves through the inculcation of habitus, which might imply a rather static conception of the social class structure. However, he overcomes the problem of social change through the notion of *class trajectory*.

Hospitality, Leisure & Tourism Series

This notion is used in two different ways: to explain the movement of a class or a class fraction upwards or downwards in the hierarchy and to explain an individual's progress through a life history. The notion of class trajectory explains why certain fractions of social classes may veer towards the tastes of another class. This may occur, for example, because there is movement in the field of economic production (and therefore possession of economic capital) which either encourages a class fraction to adopt pretensions for the future or which forces a class fraction to adapt to shifting forms of capital. These shifting forms of capital constitute new sites of struggle and new class fractions. In terms of an individual's trajectory, Bourdieu points out that it is possible, for example, to distinguish the children of the old bourgeoisie from those who have recently arrived by their familiarity and ease with cultural capital:

> (cultural capital) opposes … those … who acquired their cultural capital by early daily contact with rare 'distinguished' things, people, places and shows, to those who owe their capital to an acquisitive effort directed by the educational system … whose relationship to it is more serious, more severe, often more tense. (Bourdieu, 1984, p. 127).

The lack of ease experienced by individuals whose trajectory changes in this way is often revealed by a reversion to the tastes and practices of the original class habitus when in private. Food tastes and practices in particular, argues Bourdieu, often reveal the deepest dispositions of the habitus. Thus we may observe a return to the heavier, fattier foods of childhood habitus when in private among those individuals who have adopted the ascetic eating habits of the professional class fraction of the dominating classes while in public.

This section has explored Bourdieu's ideas about the relationship between class and taste. For Bourdieu, taste is not only socially constructed but it is constructed through membership of a particular habitus located in the hierarchy of class relationships. In the struggle for legitimacy, status and power, the expression of taste becomes a way of establishing claims to distinction. However, these expressions of taste and the particular social practices that embody them are not static. As the material conditions of existence change and more class fractions have access to the cultural and symbolic capital that signifies superiority, so the dominant classes shift their tastes and preferences to ensure distance between themselves and the dominated classes. Food tastes and practices are a particularly good vehicle for expressing these social distinctions and judgements and derive from habitus and class.

Alternative explanations of the social construction of taste

The notion that the primary influence on the social construction of taste is social class has come under heavy criticism in recent years. Bourdieu, in particular, has been criticized on many grounds, most of them related to the view that a class analysis of taste (or anything else) is outdated in modern society[3] and/or is not relevant outside of France. One set of arguments suggests that tastes have become standardized as the result of a process of levelling down of culture generally and the processes of rationalization, democratization and industrialization. The concept of standardization thus challenges the framework put forward by Bourdieu to explain how tastes are constructed. A further set of arguments takes an almost opposite view, suggesting that we are no longer restricted by wider social structural processes such as social class (or gender or race for that matter) but that we are free to create our own identities/make choices, etc. This can be linked to a body of thinking called postmodernism. In some versions of this stream of thought individuals are not conceived of as completely atomized and rootless but as members of shifting groups and alliances (Maffesoli, 1988), a sort of tribal society rather than an individualistic society (refer to Chapter 2 for a discussion on postmodernism).

These alternative paradigms imply contradictory conceptions of the amount of choice actually available within which we express our tastes. We turn first to a consideration of the argument that class is irrelevant to an understanding of the construction of taste because of the processes of standardization, rationalization and globalization. The paradigm of postmodernism is examined in the next chapter.

Standardization

The notion of *standardization* is linked to the concept of *massification*. This derives from a critique of mass culture where distinction of taste and culture are said to be lost in unadventurous and unimaginative products and services designed to appeal to the lowest level denominators of mass consumption. Aesthetic values and discriminating taste atrophy in the face of standardized products. The manufacturers of goods and services have an interest in producing uniform products which can be sold to a large number of people. The more uniform the product, the greater are the economies of scale which can be made and, therefore, the greater the profit on each unit sold. This is the argument of Ritzer (1996), who uses the spread of McDonalds fast food restaurants as a metaphor for the increasing standardization and rationalization of contemporary society. Such standardization produces simplified product ranges, emphasizes quantity over quality and values uniformity over experimentation (Wood, 1998). Further, as Wood (1995) points out, the variations produced to appeal to local markets (mass customization) produce only the illusion of consumer choice, since the consumer can only choose between different variants of essentially the same product. In the absence of choice, there is little opportunity for strategies of distinction based on class. Taste is socially constructed, but through the influence of suppliers of uniform food products and services.

Ritzer (2001) argues, using terminology drawn from Bourdieu, that in a highly McDonaldized society 'we can expect the habitus of most people to be endowed with a strong propensity to prefer McDonaldized settings' (Ritzer, 2001, p. 68). This is because the more that settings such as McDonalds dominate, the less there is a choice to experience other settings, and so even those whose capital predisposes them to prefer other settings will be forced into standardized settings. Ritzer does allow for some minor class-based differences, arguing that the greatest propensity to prefer standardized settings will be found among the working classes and the least among the upper classes with the middle classes somewhat ambivalent, but suggests that these differences gradually disappear as the logic of standardization spreads. However, this is a somewhat simplistic

Hospitality, Leisure & Tourism Series

reading of Bourdieu and the relationship between the different forms of capital and the development of habitus, of the relationship between class-based habitus and the formation of tastes, and of strategies of distinction. Moreover, it is by no means established that the process of McDonaldization has reached or will reach such a saturation point.[4]

Ritzer's arguments do not, of course, rest on the spread of McDonalds restaurants in particular. Fischler (1996) has pointed out that the standardization process has reached traditional restaurants, which are increasingly making use of industrialized, standardized ingredients rather than fresh ones. However, it is important not to confuse the standardization of ingredients and dishes offered in restaurants with a decrease in taste distinctions between the social classes. Fantasia (1995) examined the profile of fast food consumers in France, and notes that the category including senior managers, industrialists and professionals together made up only 7 per cent of the customers. Even more interesting is the fact that manual workers (who make up 40 per cent of the labour force) represented only 2 per cent of customers and that the lower level white collar workers (21 per cent of the labour force) provided 32 per cent of the customers (directly contradicting Ritzer's arguments discussed earlier). On the other hand the statistics do support Bourdieu's contention that the boundary marking the break with the popular relation to food runs between the manual workers and the clerical and commercial employees.

That said, by far the most striking characteristic of consumers is age, with 83 per cent of customers of fast food hamburger restaurants in France under the age of 34 and 57 per cent under 24. This has led some commentators to worry that the taste for standardized food will be more widespread in future generations (Beaujour, 2000). However, Fantasia's (1995) study found that while adolescents enjoyed the freedom from adult supervision and traditional rules represented by fast food they did not believe that they would or should take the place of the café in France. He concludes that the fast food sector and standardization does not pose a threat to the culinary establishment because 'in market terms they are sustained by a different consumer population and in cultural terms, (that) they are concerned with fundamentally different activities' (Fantasia, 1995, p. 233).

In the case of the UK, it could equally well be argued that the lower prices and the informality of standardized commercial dining, far from threatening the development of culinary taste, may instead enable its diffusion to social groups who would otherwise never eat outside the home. In countries lacking a strong cultural perception of national cuisine and gastronomic conventions, it is hard to make a case for the argument that standardization is a threat.

However, the arguments concerning the effects of standardization on the construction of taste do not rest solely on the spread of McDonalds. It is also possible to argue that the industrialization of food has standardized ingredients with a consequent impact on taste. It is difficult to appreciate taste in a world where food is standardized at the expense of taste and geographical mobility means that foods can be consumed out of their natural environment and out of season. Food writers have also commented on the way in which at the same time that consumers can buy fruit out of season, home grown varieties are disappearing. Poulain (2002) comments that very often taste falls victim to the profits of the agro-industrial companies and cites the disappearance of dozens of varieties of apples and pears, replaced by the omnipresent granny smith and golden delicious.

It is certainly true that food is now consumed out of its natural context and that a great number of tasks to do with food preparation have left the home or restaurant kitchen to be undertaken by food companies. More and more pre-prepared foods and dishes are sold in supermarkets, for example. However this does not mean in itself that distinctions of taste between the social classes have disappeared. First, those who have higher economic capital can afford to express their taste by buying expensively imported exotic ingredients.[5] Secondly some products are specifically designed to appeal to 'discerning' customers, allowing a particular class fraction to express its distinction through, for example, a taste for healthy, ascetic food or exotic aesthetic food tastes. Thirdly, as Bourdieu has noted, as soon as a product loses its exclusivity the upper classes turn away from it and search for new taste markers.[6] In all likelihood then, food purchases and tastes of all social classes change over time, but habitus and the possession of differing amounts of economic capital continue to determine the construction of taste. It is suggested (Poulain, 2002) that the taste of the upper classes in France has now changed to embrace traditional regional cuisine in restaurants (previously rejected as lacking the artistic complexity of haute cuisine) and reject industrialized standardized food. Thus it is far from evident that taste is socially constructed through the efforts of the suppliers of standardized products and services. On the contrary, the evidence supports the view that sees the taste for these products as a product of class, and the ability to appreciate non-standardized food as a mark of distinction.

Indeed there is evidence that food as a signifier of taste and distinction continues in its importance, not only in France, but in the USA (DeVault, 1991) and Britain (Warde et al., 1999). DeVault found that among the professional and managerial class fractions, families saw food, its qualities and its evaluation in aesthetic terms as an appropriate and necessary topic of conversation. Here knowledge of and ability to talk about food and restaurants appears to be an aspect of cultural capital that interacts with the acquisition of economic capital through occupational practices. As Warde points out, such accomplishments have to be acquired 'through exposure to restaurants and to information about canons of good or fashionable taste' (1997, p. 107). Warde concludes from his study of food habits that although 'style is important and (that) food is a vehicle for its expression, the evidence...suggests that collective styles of consumption persist and that these continue to be grounded socially' (Warde, 1997, p. 122). A comparison of data from 1968 and 1988 revealed continued existence of class differentiation, which leads Warde to support the class-based formulation of social taste suggested by Bourdieu. Further, in a study examining the practice of eating out in different sorts of restaurants in Britain, (Warde et al., 1999, p. 124) remark that 'experience of foreign cuisines is a mark of refinement, the possession of which is class related', and that 'cultural consumption continues to reflect social inequalities and, if it symbolizes refinement, is a potential mechanism for social exclusion'. Tomlinson (1994, 1998) shows through an analysis of food consumption statistics that social class in Britain is still expressed through distinctive food tastes. Finally, in a study of eating out, Warde and Martens

(2000, p. 80) find that social class is a determining factor in the explanations of variations in the experience of respondents. In Bourdieu's terms, a combination of economic and cultural capital determined eating out behaviour.

This chapter has set out the arguments of one of the most influential writers on the social construction of taste, Pierre Bourdieu. Bourdieu argues that taste is socially constructed rather than innate and that the primary mechanism for its construction is social class. Bourdieu has been criticized by those who argue that even if social class was once an influential factor it has lost its relevance in contemporary society; or that Bourdieu's ideas are relevant for France but not elsewhere.[7] Here one strand of the criticisms has been examined: the notion of standardization. The paradigm of standardization argues that distinctions of taste are disappearing due to the associated processes of massification, industrialization and standardization. Proponents of this point of view suggest that class-based distinctions of taste (and indeed the class hierarchy itself) are being eroded by the food suppliers, who dominate what we eat inside and outside the home and whose interests lie in providing uniform products. This argument supports the proposition that taste is socially constructed but holds that the primary determinant is the food suppliers and that what is constructed is standardized taste.

However, this chapter has argued that food tastes are far from being standardized and has presented evidence from France, Britain and the USA. It has also argued that social class is embedded in society to such an extent that standardization is unlikely to become the dominant influence on the construction of culinary taste.

End notes

1 The four forms of capital are economic, social, symbolic and cultural.
2 The three structures of consumption he examines are food, culture and presentation (clothing, beauty care, etc.). He then maps out patterns of expenditure for three fractions within the dominant class: industrial and commercial employers, teachers and members of the professions.

3 However, evidence drawn from a study of all the children born in 1946, 1958 and 1974 in Britain shows that social class remains the most important determinant of opportunities and choices. (*Guardian*, 12/10/02, report on Changing Britain, Changing Lives, 2003).

4 Of interest too is a recent article which suggests that consumers are turning away from the traditional McDonald's product. In response to falling sales, the company has introduced ... the traditional American diner with waitress service in the USA, and in Paris has upgraded its restaurants to look more like Parisian cafés. (*Guardian*, 19th September 2002, p. 28).

5 For example, the River Café cookbooks demand highly specialized expensive ingredients.

6 When the first McDonalds opened on the Champs Elysées in Paris, the bourgeoisie temporarily adopted it as 'chic'.

7 It is interesting to note how often criticisms of Bourdieu lack any convincing evidence. See, for example, Douglas, 1996, pp. 29–32.

Bibliography

Alfino, M., Caputo, J.S. and Wynyard, R. (1998). *McDonaldization Revisited: Critical Essays on Consumer Culture*. Westport: Praeger.

Beaujour, A. (2000). Pour résister au goût unique. *L'Express*. 12/10/00.

Bourdieu, P. (1979). *La distinction. Critique Social du Jugement*. Paris: Les Editions de Minuit.

Bourdieu, P. (1984). *Distinction: A Social Critique of the Judgement of Taste*. London: Routledge and Kegan Paul.

Bourdieu, P., Darbel, A. and Schnapper, D. (1991). *The Love of Art: European Art Museums and their Public*. Cambridge: Polity press.

DeVault, M. (1991). *Feeding the Family: The Social Organisation of Caring as Gendered Work*. Chicago: University of Chicago Press.

Elias, N. (1978). *The Civilising Process: The History of Manners*. Oxford: Blackwell.

Fantasia, R. (1995). Fast food in France. *Theory and Society* **24**, 201–243.

Fischler, C. (1993). *L'(h)omnivore: Le Goût, la Cuisine et le Corps.* Paris: Editions Odile Jacob.

Fischler, C. (1996). La 'Mcdonaldisation' des Moeurs. In *L'histoire de l'alimentation* (J.L. Flandrin, M. Monyanari and C. Fischler, Eds). Paris: Fayard.

Maffesoli, M. (1988). *Le Temps des Tribus, le Declin de l'individualisme dans les Sociétés de Masse.* Méridiens Klincksieck.

Poulain, J-P. (2002). *Sociologies de l'alimentation.* Paris: Presses Universitaires de France.

Ritzer, G. (1996). *The McDonaldization of Society,* rev. ed. London: Pine Forge.

Ritzer, G. (2001). *Explorations in the Sociology of Consumption.* London: Sage Publications.

Scholliers, P. (2001). *Food, Drink and Identity.* Oxford: Berg.

Tomlinson, M. (1994). Do distinct class preferences for foods exist? *British Food Journal* **96** (7), 11–17.

Tomlinson, M. (1998). Changes in tastes in Britain. *British Food Journal* **100** (6), 295–301.

The Guardian (2002). Turmoil Underneath the Arches. 19 September.

Warde, A. (1997). *Consumption, Food and Taste.* London: Sage Publications.

Warde, A., Martens, L. and Olsen, W. (1999). Consumption and the problem of variety: cultural omnivorousness, social distinction and dining out. *Sociology* **33** (1), 105–127.

Warde, A. and Martens, L. (2000). *Eating Out: Social Differentiation, Consumption and Pleasure.* Cambridge: Cambridge University Press.

Wilkes, C. (1990). Bourdieu's Class. In *An Introduction to the Work of Pierre Bourdieu* (R. Harker, C. Mahar and C. Wilkes, Eds). Houndmills: Macmillan.

Wood, R.C. (1995). *The Sociology of the Meal.* Edinburgh: Edinburgh University Press.

Wood, R.C. (1998). 'Old wine in new bottles: critical limitations of the McDonaldisation Thesis; the case of Hospitality services'. In *McDonaldisation Revisited: Critical Essays on Consumer Culture* (M. Alfino, J. Caputo and R. Wynyard, Eds). Praeger.

2

The postmodern palate: dining out in the individualized era

Donald Sloan

There exists a popular assumption that our taste, expressed through the clothes we wear, the music we listen to and of course the restaurants in which we dine, is reflective of our truly individual personalities. This chapter evaluates whether that is indeed the case. Are we free to construct our own self-identities that we display through our consumer behaviour, or alternatively, are we essentially the products of our social environments?

Postmodernism

The term postmodernism is now ubiquitous. It is commonly used within and beyond academic discourse and its scope of application seems almost limitless. Despite a recurring suggestion that the term is actually meaningless, that it is a false construct perpetuated by self-serving intellectuals, it does seem that commentary on postmodernism has helped us to articulate the nature of contemporary cultural developments (Featherstone, 1991, p. 1).

The task of defining postmodernism as an identifiable social phenomenon is disrupted by the implication inherent within the prefix 'post'. As Featherstone notes:

> The problem with the term … [postmodernism] … revolves around the question of when does a term defined oppositionally to, and feeding off an established term start to signify something substantially different. (Featherstone, 1991, p. 7)

An understanding of the term can, it would seem, only come from being able to identify aspects of contemporary society that are discernibly different from that which went before, and from observing the processes of societal change.

The modern era is usually identified as the period during which mass industrialization occurred, as did supportive systems of national government and social infrastructure. At the heart of sociological commentary on the modern era has been an analysis of class-based social hierarchies and of their role in supporting industrial institutions. Indeed, as Beck notes (1992, p. 10), our acceptance of theories of modernity has resulted in us being accustomed to only consider social structures within the context of industrial structures. Sociological theories of modernity emphasize homogeneity and suggest that models of societal construction are universally applicable. In contrast, commentary on postmodernism rejects universally applicable propositions on the dynamics of contemporary society, on issues such as social class and power, and favours instead 'local narratives' (Calhoun et al., 2002, p. 414), which reveal the supposedly changing, unstructured nature of our present day life. However, this observation does not, in itself, display whether postmodernists have done more than comment upon forms of behaviour that are evident within the latter stages of the modern era, rather than having established a new and significantly different sociological theory.

In his seminal text, 'Risk Society – Towards a New Modernity', Beck (1992) observes the changing nature of late twentieth-century capitalist society. At the centre of his thesis is his claim that traditional social hierarchies, which were both reflective of and supportive of divisions in the industrial labour market, are diminishing in importance. As he states:

> At that point [1950s] in time the unstable unity of shared life experiences mediated by the market and shaped by status, which Max Weber brought together in the concept of social class, began to break apart. Its different elements (such as material conditions dependent upon specific market opportunities, the effectiveness of tradition and of pre-capitalist lifestyles, the consciousness of communal bonds and of barriers to mobility, as well as networks of contact) have slowly disintegrated. (Beck, 1992, p. 96)

Beck's consideration of the consequences of this perceived change in the structure of society centres on the concept of *reflexive modernity* (1992) which, he suggests, requires us to develop our own biographies without the guiding influence of traditional class frameworks (termed *industrial modernity*). This process, known as *individualization*, encourages a belief that social legitimacy stems from personal achievement and the fulfilment of ambition, which in turn enhances the likelihood of individualized crises.

In addition, individualization diminishes the established characteristics and influence of social class groups, which normally had political roots. New political alliances have become issue based, rather than having a broad social class foundation. This results in temporary 'coalitions' (Beck, 1992, p. 100) of those with an interest in current campaigns and causes, often which are picked up and publicized by the media. The only permanent group conflicts, Beck (1992, p. 101) suggests, emerge from our '... ascribed characteristics ... ', which are 'Race, skin color, gender, ethnicity, age, homosexuality, physical disabilities ... ' Groups that are formed on the basis of such ascribed characteristics now seek to gain political influence through highlighting the incompatibility of group inequality with contemporary achievement orientation.

Zygmunt Bauman, one of the most prolific and distinguished commentators on postmodernism, who actually highlighted the supposed demise of the class-based system prior to Beck, dwells on the consequences of societal change for the individual. He reflects (2001) upon the extent to which individuals' self-identities, throughout the modern era, were set by an unquestioned governing framework. It was, he suggests, the acceptance of such a framework, and its perpetuation through acceptance, which enabled us to attach meaning to our life choices. In addition, life meanings that we gained through forming connections with cultural phenomenon which were not ephemeral, but which were considered eternal, were not considered to be of equal value and so helped maintain social hierarchies. Bauman also highlights the view, often expressed by those that might be considered *mainstream* sociologists, that the constancy of the societal framework and the life meanings that it imposed, were maintained through the ideological hegemony of one social class. Readers will note that this view of the dynamics of society has been refined by Pierre Bourdieu (refer to Chapter 1).

Bauman's break with the mainstream, and the most obviously controversial element of his thesis, comes with his assertion that this view of the organization of society, and its resultant influence on life choices and self-identity formation, is now becoming redundant. In its place he sees emerging a society in which individuals' face insecurity and potential isolation as they are operating outwith the familiarity of reasoned conditions and boundaries. As he states:

> I propose that sociality, habitat, self-constitution and self-assembly should occupy in the sociological theory of post-modernity the central place that the orthodoxy of modern social theory reserved for the categories of society, normative group (like class or community), socialization and control. (Bauman, 2002, p. 432)

In Bauman's vision of society, the apparent deconstruction of established frameworks, which had the power to set behavioural norms, forces us to seek an alternative. This comes in the form of a range of relatively autonomous habitats, which we approach and accept or reject on a trial and error basis, which provide us with a 'self-assembly pattern'. Our freedom of access to different habitats, and therefore our ability to determine our self-assembly patterns is of course limited, and it is this that forms the basis of inequality in contemporary life. Our accumulation of appropriate 'symbolic tokens' (2002, p. 434), which provide access to habitats and increase our range of realistic life choices, which in turn facilitate opportunities to develop our personal identities and social standing, is dependent upon our knowledge of the behavioural traits required within each habitat.

It should be clear that neither Beck nor Bauman are proposing that postmodernism signifies the emergence of a democratized society in which changes in the source of social status, and the consequential inequalities stemming from the cultural dominance of certain groups, have been overcome. Inequality is still evident, they suggest, but is increasingly based on factors other than social class.

Postmodern consumerism and self-identity

As Warde (1990) notes, patterns of consumption have not traditionally been a focus of attention for sociologists, unless in relation to manufacturing industry or social ills such as addiction or famine. However, much sociological enquiry does now centre on the extent to which the apparent disintegration of socio-economic class divisions and our resultant membership of alternative cultural habitats are linked with our consumer behaviour. In essence, are our self-identities now formed and displayed less through our occupations and positions in the class hierarchy, and more through our understanding and acceptance of the symbolic value of goods and services?

A useful starting point for this element of the discussion is to note the apparent changing status of the consumer. There now seems to be widespread acceptance that in the developed world we are living in 'consumer societies', whether or not this is a term that is commonly understood. Reflective of this is that the word 'consumer' no longer applies only to those buying products from retail outlets, but also to:

> Museum visitors, theatre audiences, sports spectators and T.V. viewers; university students, social workers' clients and even taxpayers and the public served by the police. (Abercrombie et al., 1994, p. 1)

What is implied by the scope of application of the term is that those providing any form of service, whether in the commercial or public sectors, should adopt an explicit 'customer orientation'. This could be taken to signify that the status of the consumer, or as Abercrombie et al. (1994) suggest the 'authority' of the consumer, has grown.

In his review of the literature on theories of postmodern consumer culture, Featherstone (1991) identifies complementary themes: the growing significance of the symbolic value of goods and services; the aestheticization of everyday life; and the emergence of 'lifestyle culture'.

In relation to the first of these themes, the rapid expansion in the scale of capitalist production, which has occurred since the 1950s, has resulted in consumption becoming a key element of leisure activity. This might signify the dawning of an egalitarian, democratized culture, or, through the eyes of the more cynical observer, it may stem from mass manipulation of consumers by sophisticated capitalist organizations. Of course these two alternative views are not necessarily mutually exclusive. Featherstone (1991) examines the consequences of the growth in the scale of consumer activity, including whether it signifies some deeper change in the structure and organization of society. He draws on the work of Baudrillard, who has used semiotic analysis in an attempt to comprehend the symbolic meaning of modern commodities and consumer experiences. In line with postmodernist thought, in Baudrillard's latter works (Poster, 2001), he proposes that metannaratives, which suggest a structure to society that places us in continuously evolving historical contexts, are no longer relevant. Instead, he holds that we are operating in a 'virtual' or 'hyper-real' (Poster, 2001) world in which our sense of reality is derived from media-generated images. The images (or signs) emanating from and associated with commodities, most often generated by advertisers, provide our operating context. As Baudrillard states:

> Advertising [...] is mass society, which, with the aid of an arbitrary and systematic sign, induces receptivity, mobilizes consciousness, and reconstitutes itself in the very process as the collective. (Baudrillard, 2001, p. 13)

It is our 'receptivity' to the profusion and presentation of commodities and images that stimulates desire:

> Streets with overcrowded and glittering store windows, the displays of delicacies, and all the scenes of alimentary

and vestimentary festivity, stimulate a magical salivation. (Baudrillard, 2001, p. 33)

At the core of the second theme identified by Featherstone (1991) is a suggestion that in postmodern society our tastes, preferences and consumer choices are now, more than ever before, influenced by aesthetic considerations. Featherstone (1991) tracks the manner in which everyday life has become increasingly aestheticized. The foundations of this trend were laid by the urban flaneurs of the mid-nineteenth century who sought, through their personal conduct, to turn their lives into works of art. In the UK this approach was exemplified in the life of Oscar Wilde, who '... we remember ... as much for what he was as for what he wrote ... ' (Eagleton, 1991, p. vii). It might be safe to assume that the words of Lord Illingworth, a character in Wilde's play *A Woman of no Importance*, were reflective of Wilde's personal ambitions:

> A man who can dominate a London dinner table can dominate the world. The future belongs to the dandy. It is the exquisites who are going to rule. (Russell, 1989, p. 62)

Later, in the 1960s, the aestheticization of everyday life was further propelled by the emergence of pop art, the greatest proponent of which was Andy Warhol. His success in challenging established notions of what constitutes art, partly through creating works that centred on unremarkable and accessible consumer goods, such as tins of Campbell's soup, and on icons of popular culture, such as Marilyn Monroe, encouraged the masses to indulge in aesthetic judgement, a pastime that was previously the preserve of the cultural elite. This can be seen as part of a wider trend that undermined the authority of those who previously had the exclusive right to determine what was, and was not, of cultural significance. For some this was interpreted as a depressing descent towards the granting of credibility to popular culture. For others, such as Angela Robbie, it was:

> ... the coming into being of those whose voices were historically drowned out by the (modernist) metanarratives of mastery, which were in turn both patriarchal and imperialist (1994, p. 23, cited in Storey, 1999, p. 133) which

> ... has enfranchised a new body of intellectuals, voices
> from margins speaking from positions of difference: ethnic,
> gender, class, sexual preference ... (Storey, 1999, p. 133)

Such trends, in addition to the evident blurring of the distinction between art and design, is leading to widespread '... aesthetic consumption and the need [for the individual] to form life into an aesthetically pleasing whole ... ' (Featherstone, 1991, p. 67). This may add weight to Baudrillard's (2001) proposal that we are operating in a hyper-real world and also, as is commonly suggested, that as our contemporary preoccupation with aesthetics is fuelled by media output then it is based on little more than ephemeral values, the consequence of which is that our cultural markers do not relate to history or tradition, and our lives lack depth.

The challenge that comes to us all, in a world in which we are faced with a profusion of images and a vast array of consumer choices, the implications of which can be symbolically and emotionally significant, is to steer a path that enables us to create appealing lifestyles. Lifestyle, based on consumer preferences, is the primary means by which we communicate to others the nature of our desired self-perception. As Featherstone notes:

> The modern individual within consumer culture is made
> conscious that he speaks not only with his clothes, but
> with his home, furnishings, decoration, car and other
> activities which are to be read and classified in terms of
> the presence and absence of taste. (Featherstone,
> 1991, p. 86)

This might imply that individuals have absolute freedom to pursue personal pleasures, and indeed Featherstone accepts that the desire to develop a lifestyle is not the preserve of members of only particular groups, but is a possibility for many, regardless of age or sex. However, he does suggest that similar lifestyles are evident within class fractions, rather than the widespread desire for lifestyle acquisition signifying that we are entering a more egalitarian age. In essence, he proposes that we are all more lifestyle conscious, yet our lifestyle construction is still greatly influenced by traditional social frameworks. Clearly this challenges key aspects of the postmodernist case.

By whatever means consumer behaviour may be influenced it is certainly the case that we make judgements about others based on our analysis of lifestyles. As Storey notes (1999), when we meet someone new, our understanding of their character comes from observations about their lifestyle, which in turn comes from questioning them about their patterns of consumption:

> On knowing the answer to enough of these questions [relating to their consumer behaviour], we feel able to construct a cultural and social pattern and thus to begin to locate the person in a particular cultural and social space – we begin, in other words, to think we know who they are. (Storey, 1999, p. 128)

Despite the importance that is placed on the act of consumption, in particular on its ability to reveal aspects of personal character, there is no suggestion from Storey that our consumption patterns actually:

> ... determine our social being; but it does mean that what we consume provides us with a script with which we can stage and perform in a variety of ways, the drama of who we are. (Storey, 1999, p. 136)

For Storey, like so many others, our social being, which as he suggests is reflected in our cultural consumption, is greatly influenced by traditional forms of social stratification.

For Bauman too, consumption is a reflection of self, but as was noted earlier in this chapter he is one of relatively few sociologists who suggests that traditional social hierarchies do not now greatly influence the construction of self. He proposes that despite not having total authority, the postmodern consumer has drawn power away from the cultural and professional elites which previously controlled access to certain service environments and cultural experiences. It is the absence of normative cultural frameworks and the inevitable control which they exercised, which casts us adrift and provides us with the freedom to develop self-identities through consumption (Warde, 1994). What we are witnessing, Bauman suggests (2002, p. xv) is a new requirement for self-determination rather than experiencing socially constructed determination. An important aspect of this personal quest for identity formation, as a consequence of individualization, is that it is an ongoing process or journey. As Bauman states:

> … individualization consists in transforming human identity from a given into a task – and charging the actors with the responsibility for performing that task and for the consequences (also the side effects of their performance). (Bauman, 2002, p. xv)

Or, as Storey succinctly puts it: identity formation is less about 'roots' and more about 'routes' (1999, p. 135). The continuous nature of the process of identity formation means that individuals who are 'disembedded' can have no destination in which they become 'reembedded' (Bauman, 2002, p. xvi) and where they might find contentment and satisfaction. In addition, the independent nature of the journey is fraught with risk as personal success, as well as failure, is self-generated. If we accept this element of Bauman's argument then we might conclude that despite the emancipation and personal empowerment which individualization can bring, so too it brings its own pressures to bare. A pessimistic interpretation of the consequences of individualization might also suggest that it breeds widespread indifference to others and undermines any sense of wider community.

Bauman examines the relationship between consumption, identity formation and changing social structures in some detail. He accepts that access to the market is limited and in this respect he distinguishes between the *seduced* and the *repressed* (Warde, 1994). The seduced are those who indulge in consumption and whose primary motive for doing so is the formation of self-identity. Individual freedom of choice characterizes the existence of the seduced. They are not restricted by socialization, nor do they suffer from intrusive state regulation. There is a risk, however, that the seduced may experience anxiety and even a sense of isolation resulting from the individual rather than collective nature of their responsibility for making consumer choices. However, any anxiety may be assuaged, Bauman suggests (Warde, 1994), through reliance on expert advice, most probably from the advertising industry. In contrast, the repressed are those whose freedom is limited both by poverty and state control. The repressed do not operate in the free market but rather are dependent upon the state for the provision of benefits and services.

Warde (1994) does highlight what he feels are significant weaknesses within Bauman's case. These can be summarized as follows:

- While Bauman does propose that there exists harmless competition between consumers over the acquisition of self-identities (harmless because competition is not reflective of unappealing societal divisions), this underplays the extent to which consumption can be driven for a desire for perceived social and cultural supremacy, often through displays of conspicuous consumption (Warde, 1997).

- Although there is no doubt that identity formation is an important consideration within consumer choices, it is wrong to dismiss consumers' consideration of price, value for money and use-value. Warde (1997) points to the work of the Consumers' Association in the UK, which acts on behalf of around one million members who require information about products and services, including the results of performance tests, which they use to make rational purchase decisions.

- Bauman's rigid categorization of the seduced and the repressed is somewhat simplistic as in reality what exists is a continuum at one end of which are the wealthy and at the other end the poor. An identifiable dividing point on this continuum, in the manner in which Bauman implies, would be impossible to locate. In addition, Bauman exaggerates the extent to which the State and the market represent opposing forces of control and freedom respectively. For example, State regulation plays an important role in the smooth operation of the market, and the State does not deliberately seek to undermine the repressed, which it is likely to view as '... expensive and embarrassing ... ' (Warde, 1994, p. 60).

- The power of socialization as an influence on consumer choice is greatly underplayed. Bauman's vision of individuals operating in relative isolation, outwith well-established social networks, does not reflect common experience. Warde suggests that in addition to searching for self-identity,

'Rather more often, being socially acceptable is the goal and the means of allaying anxiety' (1994, p. 65).

Proposals from some, based on observations of consumer behaviour, incorporate an acceptance of the disintegration of rigid class hierarchies with a suggestion that new social ties are emerging. *Informalization* is characterized by a lack of conformity not only to traditional patterns of consumption but also to those that might, in a postmodern environment, be interpreted as bestowing cultural value. 'Free rein is thus given to personal preference as moral, aesthetic and social standards are relaxed, so behaviour becomes irregular ... ' (Warde, 1997, p. 13). Informalization is identified as leading to a counter tendency to individualization as those who lack association with others seek to develop new communities, a sense of belonging and connection with less transient cultural markers (*communification*). A form of communification that has consumption at its core is *stylization*.

Deindividualized stylization

So far in this chapter class-based social construction has been identified as the only credible alternative to the view, as expressed by Bauman, Beck and others, that society is now witnessing a process of individualization. However, while accepting the proposal that traditional hierarchies are becoming redundant, other postmodernists are not wedded to the concept of individualization. For example, Maffesoli (1996) starts from the premise that traditional social construction, linked to political ideologies, is being challenged. He suggests that it is appropriate to draw conclusions only after examining the nature of people's life experiences, rather than to make assumptions about life experiences based on beliefs about class hierarchies. He seems frustrated by the apparently common rejection of any view of society as being heterogeneous. However, rather than accepting individualization as a dominant trend he proposes that a process of deindividualization is resulting in the emergence of new forms of social group, or 'tribe'. Maffesoli (1996) suggests that we too readily accept and rely on the concept of individualization, as is evident in academic and journalistic commentary, and that we promote it as the cause of a supposed decline in collectivism and a growth in levels of selfishness. He presents such an approach as lazily conventional and suggests that it masks the nature of contemporary social ties. As he states:

> We have dwelled so often on the dehumanization and the disenchantment with the modern world and the solitude it induces that we are no longer capable of seeing the networks of solidarity that exist within. (Maffesoli, 1996, p. 72)

Rather than our identities being self-contained, Maffesoli suggests that the reality of our existence comes from social interaction. He examines the extent to which such interaction results in the formation of tribes and the influence of interaction within tribes. In essence, he believes that we become members of various tribes, each of which might relate to some aspect of our lives (e.g. youth culture, hobbies and musical preferences), and within which we accept and contribute to the evolution of shared values, attitudes and tastes. It is the fluidity (multiple membership and movement between tribes) and its consequences, which might incorrectly be taken to signify ongoing individualization, rather than complex socialization. In Maffesoli's opinion, a crucial element of this system of tribes is that public expressions of membership, through the adoption of conspicuous lifestyles, are becoming increasingly common.

The term stylization (Warde, 1997) describes an apparent growing preoccupation with style consciousness as a central aspect of lifestyle, and it is suggested by some (e.g. Maffesoli, 1996) that the development of lifestyle is increasingly becoming an end in itself. Within style groups a system of codes exist which are used to maintain exclusivity and set criteria for membership. There is a risk that in developing a commentary on rising levels of style-consciousness, and its expression through consumption, we might lose track of the question of influence. Are members of style groups bound by pursuit of a lifestyle for reasons unrelated to class-based political ideologies? There is a suggestion that a tendency towards style consciousness is more evident within certain socially marginal communities, the members of which possibly feel isolated from wider society. Empirical work undertaken by Haslop et al. (1998) suggests

Hospitality, Leisure & Tourism Series

that members of a particular gay community (those frequenting bars and nightclubs in Manchester's 'gay village') are not bound by modernist conventions. As they state:

> From a postmodernist marketing perspective, the 'gay market' is of considerable interest, as it is not organically based on a particular location of historical community, but is a portmanteau term for people from all walks of life who share a form of sexual identity, which they choose to make visible to varying degrees, depending on preference, mood and external conditions. (Haslop et al., 1998, p. 319)

Haslop et al. go on to examine the role that common style traits play within this community. They note that the 'double burden of stigma and invisibility' (1998, p. 319) has encouraged many to adopt shared patterns of consumption, expressed through style, that act as a form of communication; communication of group membership, of distinction from wider society, and of acceptance of particular values. It is suggested that a semiotic code is established, primarily based on aspects of lifestyle, which facilitates an unspoken understanding between group members and which provides a welcome sense of security. It is claimed that a crucial element of consumption for this community centres on the shared social spaces in which adopted lifestyles are acted out, most commonly pubs and nightclubs. They are not simply centres of consumption. They influence those who attend through a process of cultural socialization and therefore become the forum in which to learn the cultural norms of the community and through which to secure membership.

Lugosi and Peacock (2000) highlight another specific social group for whom norms of social consumption have become established which, in turn, influence aspects of lifestyle for individual members. They studied behaviour evident within particular clubs that serve, almost exclusively, those involved in London's West-end theatre productions. They witnessed wildly hedonistic yet stylized behaviour, the like of which would be considered unacceptable in many circles, but which in these environments was positively encouraged. They conclude that distinctive, stylized behaviour of those from this artistic community is used to signify membership, perpetuate distinction and provide a form of comfort and security.

In both these examples, there is a suggestion that the emphasis on style in patterns of consumption actually has a democratizing effect. It can conceal divisions that may once have been at the fore, such as those based on class, by imposing a new range of cultural conventions. These conventions rest upon an understanding and display of style.

It is worth considering whether democratization of this sort extends beyond those within specific minority groups. Mort (1996) comments on the extent to which the rising importance of lifestyle in the UK was directly linked to the tax cutting policies of the Thatcher government during the 1980s. He notes that there was a widespread perception among the government's opponents that tax cuts, which fuelled excessive consumption, were responsible for the emergence of shallow and transient value systems within which the role of lifestyle became central. As he states:

> the government has spawned a 'candy floss society' in which consumer spending had been allowed to run riot. The worship of money [and the] uncontrollable demand for goods, was forging a new civilization of banality. (Mort, 1996, p. 2)

In addition, and with echoes of some postmodern commentary, Mort claims that the government explicitly promoted the view that the growth in consumerism brought freedom from the shackles of the class-bound society.

> The rhetoric of the marketplace, which equated the freedom to spend money with broader political and cultural freedoms, was identified as a key part of this political vocabulary. (Mort, 1996, p. 5)

However, despite the claims of the political masters of the time, it is difficult to find empirical evidence that supports the view that consumerism, and its expression through lifestyle, brings emancipation. The growth in both style conscientiousness and political apathy do not in themselves suggest freedom from class boundaries.

Dining out

At this stage in the chapter readers could be forgiven for questioning how this commentary relates to culinary taste and consumer behaviour in the restaurant sector. Well, there can be few types of venue in which the style conscious come out to play quite so conspicuously as in restaurants. Evidence suggests that commercial hospitality spaces, including restaurants, are important centres for the display of lifestyles and for learning lifestyle conventions. It could be argued that restaurants, and the consumer behaviour which they help to sustain, are symbols of our shift to a postmodern society in which the pursuit of lifestyle is a widespread preoccupation.

Urry (1995) argues that the social role of space, and in this instance we will obviously apply our observations to the social roles of restaurants, is an issue on which there has been little serious commentary. This, he feels, is a significant omission as evidence suggests that changes in the use of space in recent years are reflective of the economic restructuring which characterizes postmodernism. Urry makes some specific observations about the changing use of space and its link with postmodernism. Firstly, as was noted earlier in this chapter, there has been an apparent growth in aesthetic culture in which visual considerations are key. Urry suggests that architecture and interior design are now less representative of cultural hegemony and moral authority and more driven by a desire to reflect and/or influence popular aesthetic appeal. Also, our preoccupation with aesthetic considerations becomes self-perpetuating as it puts more competitive pressure on the owners and operators of public spaces to make them as physically appealing as possible to customers and other stakeholders. In addition, Urry claims that our perception of the purpose of postmodern public spaces is that not only should they be aesthetically stimulating, but also that they should facilitate consumption. As he notes, the use of many spaces, especially in our cities, has changed from being production based to consumption based.

Secondly, the growth in our symbolic culture, which is largely perpetuated by the media, encourages the use of space as a forum for the development and expression of lifestyle and self-identity. Indeed as Urry suggests:

> ... it is possible for localities to consume one's identity so that such places become almost literally all-consuming places. (Urry, 1995, p. 2)

Finkelstein (1989) in her text Dining Out: a sociology of modern manners, which is still one of the most fluent examinations of the social purpose of restaurants, discusses the role of the individual within the social context. As she states:

> ... it is the convergence of the private with the public and social which designates the restaurant as an appropriate setting for a sociological analysis of contemporary habits of everyday life. (Finkelstein, 1989, p. 3)

At the heart of her argument is her belief that the restaurant is an 'architect of desire' (1989, p. 3). By this she means that the restaurant is responsible for the manufacture of expectations of particular pleasurable emotional experiences. This it does through the display of stylized and fashionable environments, the symbolic value of which is understood and valued by potential customers. In essence, she suggests that emotions have become comodified as the restaurant itself prescribes them.

Finkelstein suggests that the nature of control over social interaction between restaurant customers results in 'uncivilized sociality'. While customers might believe that restaurant dining provides the ideal opportunity for expressions of individuality, certainly within the realms of culinary taste, they are in fact adhering to stylized conventions.

Urry (1995) suggests that our understanding of stylized conventions, and their appropriateness for particular public settings (which could include restaurants) comes from a process of cultural socialization, which is often fuelled by media output. In this respect, it is worth commenting briefly on the nature of media coverage of restaurant dining and matters of culinary taste. As Randall (2000) notes, in the UK there has been a significant growth in recent years in media interest in culinary taste and dining. Randall notes that in postmodern society it is to a large extent mediated messages, from a range of genres, which influence our perceptions of food and drink related issues. She uses semiotic analysis to interpret meanings presented through media output. To an extent Randall's conclusions suggest that the current popularity of food and dining related media has as much to do with the acquisition of admired and valued lifestyles as it does with a genuine interest in cuisine. Randall highlights a number of techniques which

Hospitality, Leisure & Tourism Series

are used by the media to form influential relationships with audiences. These include celebrity chefs adopting informal styles of communication to promote a sense of intimacy with audience members. This in turn legitimizes the lifestyle which the chefs are seen to represent, of which restaurant dining and displays of good taste are important elements. Secondly, the desirability of association with the lifestyles that are supposedly adopted by celebrity chefs is further encouraged by their celebrity status. Finally, Randall notes that a significant proportion of media output, which is ostensively food and drink related, actually dwells on other issues, often related to lifestyle. For example, the popular restaurant critic A.A. Gill, of the Sunday Times newspaper, is well known for commenting upon a range of issues, such as his own lifestyle and tastes, before he begins to offer criticism of the food which he is served. This example of his work, relating to an Oxford-based restaurant that has since closed, displays how he uses rather contentious humour to maintain the interest of his readers:

> Let's start with the room. It appears to have been designed by a committee from the Women's Institute who couldn't agree on a theme .... The whole edifice screams of provincial cul-de-sac showing off, and the sort of Buddha-like suburban self-satisfaction that makes us city boys snort with patronizing derision. (Sunday Times, 05/08/01)

Conclusion

The purpose of this chapter has been to examine the concept of postmodernism and to consider its influence on culinary taste and associated consumer behaviour, particularly as expressed within the international restaurant sector. The main tenet of postmodernism is that traditional, class-based social structures, which had the power to influence social conventions, are being deconstructed. Two alternative propositions have been discussed. Firstly, that the emergence of postmodern society has resulted in individuals being free to construct their own self-identities through consumption. Secondly, that the decline of traditional social structures forces us to adopt alternative forms of social interaction and security, primarily though the adoption of lifestyles. Evidence from the restaurant sector seems to suggest that culinary taste, and associated consumer behaviour, could be considered important aspects of lifestyle. Restaurants provide environments in which to learn stylized forms of behaviour, and in which to seek membership of stylized groups. In addition, media output reinforces the lifestyle enhancing opportunities that restaurants provide. Culinary taste, it would seem, is not an expression of individual preference, but a signifier of longing for social acceptance.

Bibliography

Abercrombie, N., Keat, R. and Whiteley, N. (1994). *The Authority of the Consumer*. London: Routledge.

Adam, B., Beck, U. and Van Loon, J. (Eds) (2000). *The Risk Society and Beyond – Critical Issues for Social Theory*. London: Sage Publications.

Baudrillard, J. (2001). *Selected Writing*. Cambridge: Polity Pres.

Bauman, Z. (2001). *The Individualized Society*. Cambridge: Polity Press.

Bauman, Z. (2002). *A Sociological Theory of Postmodernism*. In *Contemporary Sociological Theory* (C. Calhoun, J. Gerteis, J. Moody, S. Pfaff and I. Vink, Eds). Maldin: Blackwell Publishing.

Beck, U. (1992). *Risk Society – Towards a New Modernity*. London: Sage Publications.

Calhoun, C., Gerteis, J., Moody, J., Pfaff, S. and Vink, I. (Eds) (2002). *Contemporary Sociological Theory*. Oxford: Blackwell Publishing.

Eagleton, T. (Ed.) (1991). *Oscar Wilde – Plays, Prose, Writings and Poems*. London: Everyman's Library.

Featherstone, M. (1987). Lifestyle and consumer culture. *Theory, Culture and Society* **4**, 55–70.

Featherstone, M. (1990). Perspectives on consumer culture. *Sociology* **24** (1), 5–22.

Featherstone, M. (1991). *Consumer Culture and Postmodernism*. London: Sage Publications.

Finkelstein, J. (1989). *Dining Out – A Sociology of Modern Manners*. Cambridge: Polity Press.

Haslop, C., Hill, H. and Schmidt, R.A. (1998). The gay lifestyle – spaces for a subculture of consumptions. *Marketing Intelligence and Planning* **16** (5), 318–326.

Hospitality, Leisure & Tourism Series

Keat, R., Whiteley, N. and Abercrombie, N. (Eds) (1994). *The Authority of the Consumer*. London: Routledge.

Lash, S. and Friedman, J. (Eds) (1992). *Modernity and Identity*. Oxford: Blackwell Publishers.

Lugosi, P. and Peackcock, M. (2000). *Inside or Out: Consumer Satisfaction and the Appropriation of Social Space in Hospitality Consumption*. In *Consumer Satisfaction Research in Tourism and Hospitality* (D. Bowen, E. Wickens, Paraskevas and N. Hemmington, Eds) Oxford: Oxford Brookes University (unpublished).

Lupton, D. (1999). *Risk*. London: Routledge.

Maffesoli, M. (1996). *The Time of the Tribes*. London: Sage Publications.

Mort, F. (1996). *Cultures of Consumption – Masculinities and Social Space in Late Twentieth-Century Britain*. London: Routledge.

Poster, M. (2001). *Selected Writings*. Cambridge: Polity Press.

Randall, S. (2000). How does the media influence public taste for food and beverage? The role of media in forming customer attitudes towards food and beverage provision. In *Strategic Questions in Food and Beverage Management* (R.C. Wood, Ed.). Oxford: Butterworth–Heinemann, pp. 81–96.

Russell, H. (Ed.) (1989). *The Sayings of Oscar Wildge*. London: Gerald Duckworth and Co. Ltd.

Storey, J. (1991). *Cultural Consumption and Everyday Life*. London: Arnold.

Urry, J. (1995). *Consuming Places*. London: Routledge.

Warde, A. (1990). Introduction to the sociology of consumption. *Sociology* **24** (1), 1–4.

Warde, A. (1994). Consumption, identity – formation and uncertainty. *Sociology* **28** (4), 877–898.

Warde, A. (1994). Consumers, identity and belonging: reflections on some theses of Zygmunt Bauman. In *The Authority of the Consumer* (R. Keat, N. Whiteley and N. Abercrombie, Eds). London: Routledge, pp. 58–74.

Warde, A. (1997). *Consumption, Food and Taste*. London: Sage Publications.

Wood, R.C. (1995). *The Sociology of the Meal*. Edinburgh: Edinburgh University Press.

Taste and space: eating out in the city today

David Bell

> Pleasure and accomplishment stem from enjoying and celebrating the specific amongst a proliferation of difference. Adopting, adapting and transforming, we can literally nourish ourselves with the diversity and constant change that characterize contemporary urban society. These are adventures in a very large kitchen.
>
> *(Miles, 1993, p. 202)*

> My cooking should represent my city, the place we live, in the ingredients but also in the culture.
>
> (Puck, 1996, p. 63)

My aim in this chapter is to think through some of the issues that the contemporary geography of urban eating out raises: the essay is not a comprehensive review of the causal links between space and taste, but instead sketches some of the practices and processes that mark Western city eating today. My motive for doing this is to provide a thinking-frame – a few catalysts for further exploration of how city living and eating out are commingled, and how that commingling illustrates broader processes at work in urban environments. The contemporary city is a space of consumption and a site of spectacle, but it is also a space of contestation, a site of refusal. Played out on the streets and plazas, the political dramas of everyday life are materialized in the practices of city living. The sociological transformations of the late modern age – all that postmodernization, deterritorialization, globalization – get worked through at the level of the everyday, the commonplace, the banal. As a concentration of these processes, eating out gives us a way into thinking through the city as a node in the disjunctive flows of contemporary culture, including global 'foodscapes' (Appadurai, 1990; Ferraro, 2002).

At the heart of my argument is the need to see contemporary cityscapes as maps of distinction, in Bourdieu's (1984) sense of the term. In analysing the taste habits of the middle classes, Bourdieu suggested a dynamic and complex dance of positional goods, moving up and down a class-inflected taste hierarchy (see also Featherstone, 1991). This process – the circulation of goods driven by the motor of cultural capital accumulation in the never-ending game of status-marking is, I want to suggest, clearly played out across urban space. Loft living, gym joining, haute cuisining: these are the habits and habitats in which distinction is most vividly mapped out (Zukin, 1995). This is a postindustrial story, of course, of cities redefining what they are once their economic base is stripped out and – if they are lucky – substituted by the symbolic economy. Place promotion, city marketing, imagineering – these are the new industries that now give shape to cities. And rising in the ranks of promotional tools in this symbolic economy is food.

The endless dance of class struggle – the struggle of manners, tastes and lifestyles – makes and remakes the metropolitan landscape as a movie set for self-presentations, for fashioning the self out of bespoke tailoring, deli counters and personal grooming. The new middle classes – taste-makers and trend-spotters *par excellence* – make fullest use of their savvy in this setting, disdaining through the subtle movements of bodies and wallets the *passé* and *déclassé*. The game is always stacked in their favour; their lifestyle journalists know it, their restaurateurs know it, their 'purveyors of fine foods' know it ... The new middle classes, as we shall see, take on the crucial role of cultural intermediaries, identified by Bourdieu as the drivers of the system of distinction. And the city is laid out before them, ripe for the tasting.

Cosmopolitan dining

The city is bountiful (as we shall see later) – it is one huge eating-out adventure, literally and figuratively, but it is not without a price: the price of exclusion, or of condescension, or of exploitation. As Hannerz (1990) has observed, the endless safari of the cosmopolitan, searching out the exotic and the authentic, is essentially a predatory practice: the pillage of resources, the scouring of habitats, the uprooting and repackaging of the foreign, the novel, the dangerous. It is summed up in an advertising slogan from British TV, to be taken only partially tongue-in-cheek: discover the world – and eat it. For a time, it was cosmopolitan enough to move outwards, to visit the Earth's four corners for new consumer choices. Now, however, the whole world has been reached and reaped, so the hunt turns inwards; more accurately, it looks to the 'other within', rediscovering (or reinventing) 'lost' (or invented) traditions, from home baking to offal eating (Visser, 1997). So, although Warde and Martens (2000, p. 91) suggest that, in the UK today, '[d]istinction is entailed in the taste for foreign food', I think this oversimplifies the relationship between 'foreignness', distinction and taste. Crucially, in a cranking-up of the dance of distinction, the quest for the 'other within' turns to habits and tastes jettisoned by the lower classes on their own upward path, as they chase the tastes of those who continually out-step them. The foods prized by the taste-makers are the same ones that, a generation ago, they sought to distance themselves from (James, 1996). A recent manifestation of this in the UK is the dramatic rise in popularity of farmers' markets, which bring to urban locales a comforting rustic nostalgia, making them a favoured haunt of new-traditionalist consumers (see for example Holloway and Kneafsey, 2000).

Farmers' markets are an interesting illustration of the broader processes I am seeking to explore here: their introduction into

Hospitality, Leisure & Tourism Series

an increasing number of UK and US city centres testifies to the ready market for their goods – and for urban consumers' quest for new culinary experiences. Culinary-cultural capital – a subspecies of Bourdieu's generalized formulation – is on display and up for grabs at these markets, as it is in many sites for urban eating. Also at work in this space, literalized in the offering of tastings by vendors, is the related practice of cultural omnivorousness.

In their sociological exploration of British urban middle-class eating out, Warde, Martens and Olsen (1999) identify this tactic of cultural omnivorousness as endemic among particular social groups, most notably the new middle classes (see also Warde and Martens, 2000). Their argument is that the potential overload of contemporary consumer culture is the cause of considerable personal anxiety: with so many products on the market, constructing a personal identity becomes fraught with unlimited choice. Out of the proliferating brands, *which one most accurately communicates who I am?* Cultural omnivorousness is thus a 'coping strategy' based on information maximization: the reassurance that comes from knowing the choices we make are as informed as we can make them. In a twist of Bourdieu's thesis that taste is used to mark distinction from other social groups, Warde et al. suggest instead that the proliferation of cultural symbols makes this kind of inter-group differentiation increasingly difficult. The complexity of the codes is such that we can never attain a decent working knowledge of the role of commodities in other social groups' identity work. In its place, taste is used as a marker of *recognition*: 'cultural judgement has its primary effect through its capacity to solidify and entrench social networks' (Warde et al. 1999, p. 124). Taste is turned inwards, to define membership rather than mark distinction – we recognize likeminds through what and where they eat, and gain comfort from the homecoming every time we walk in through the restaurant's door, and know that this is *our kind of place*. Commensality here confers equality among fellow neo-tribe members, secure in our ability to recognize shared cultural codes – a safe haven, as the antidote to the flickering confusion bombarding us when we try to make sense of others: *you are who you eat with*.

Reading between the lines of this analysis, omnivorousness starts to appear like a compulsion, a particularly middle-class eating disorder: the compulsion to eat everything, to be open to everything, to chow down on it all, in the hope that the 'best bits' can then be assembled into a new you – or, rather, *a better, more accurate reflection of the real you*. Like Hannerz's (1990) discussion of the cosmopolitan sensibility, we can see cultural omnivores as machines for taste-based self-making: omnivorousness as cultural mastery through incorporation. Only once we have processed it all can we pick those places, those plates, which say what we want them to say. The *faux pas* is to be seen dining out of place: 'ignorance of socially meaningful items might be shameful, a preference for vulgar items revealing, display of intended markers misleading, interpretation of signs mistaken' (Warde et al., 1999, p. 119). The test, as Hannerz points out, is *how far will you go to mark your social location?* What will you eat, and what remains too distasteful – either to our palates or our peers (French, 1995)? Given the anxieties of misrecognition and misinterpretation, this is a doubly tricky question, risking both a bad taste in the mouth and being marked as a person of bad taste by our peers. Negotiating these intricacies is a never-ending problem, of course, given the migration and devaluation (or strategic revaluation) of foodstuffs and eating-holes up, down and across the social (and urban) landscape. The cultural omnivores are compelled to find *all you can eat* – and to eat it – in assembling culturally legible market biographies, lifestyles and identities. So, while Midas Dekkers (2000, p. 253) is right in one sense when he says that 'people who cook a lot have more prestige than people who eat a lot', for this group, eating out is 'a perpetual experiment' (Warde and Martens, 1998, p. 120), and the (potential) source of culinary-cultural prestige.

The never-ending feast of cultural omnivorousness is facilitated – even necessitated – by the city's role as that 'very large kitchen' of which Miles writes: a site of abundance, of 'diversity and constant change' – the urban *smorgasbord*. Of course, let us not forget the poverty, the hunger, the scarcities and inadequacies – the problems of feeding the city. Abundance, however, works as a *motif*, laying out the city streets as an endless banquet, a consumer's Eden: all that choice, all those new experiences to be sought. The cultural omnivore is literalized here, eating the city, nourished by difference never-ending.

Related terms: availability, variety – food is abundant in being ever-available and always changing. The palate need never grow tired by the repetitions that marked industrial eating: the mass produced sameness spilling out of factories. That kind of abundance feeds the body but not the soul, or so it is said. Industrial food, like modernist architecture, might once have been seen as an answer to social problems, but now seems only to bring new troubles, new indigestions. Of course, abdudance-as-sameness still has a prominent place, most notably in fast foods, where it is matched by super-sizing as a double abundance. Bearing the legacy of Fordist food preparation, fast food outlets produce super-abundance and hyper-regularity, under the mantra of McDonaldization (Ritzer, 1993). This process produces the Fordist consumer, too – the McBody: 'Americans are conscripted to the unseasonable pursuit of abundance. The impossibility of the dream is saved by the translation of quality into quantity and the identification of availability with desirability' (O'Neill, 1999, p. 49). 'All you can eat' must never be *all you can eat* if you are an omnivore and not a McBody.

Abundance-as-quantity and availability-as-desirability misses so much of the distinction formula, flattening out taste to render it a predictable element. Against this there is the abundance of variety, the desirability of scarcity – or, at least, the prospect of a kind of elite scarcity that cultural capital requires. If McDonald's represents the democratization of taste, then its opposite is to be found in the paradise of the high-class food hall, or on the menu of the 'best' restaurants. Making the rare available, selectively abundant even, marks this mode of culinary production and consumption as the flipside of the drive-through super-sized McMeal. Unpredictability instead of predictability, difference rather than sameness: twin modalities of abundance that work to produce their own urban culinary geographies – twins that need each other to exist, if only to define themselves through their absolute alterity.

As part of the lifestyling of cities, key cultural intermediaries assume a prominent role. Among this taste-making group, chefs take centre-stage – the word 'stage' being particularly apt, given the slide between cooking and performance: 'In a sense, the restaurant is a forerunner of the contemporary entertainment industry' (Finkelstein, 1998, p. 203) – though lots of chefs are disdainful of the new image their profession has acquired (while often simultaneously trading on it). Moreover, the mediated image of celebrity chefs and their cooking also produces a 'pseudo-professional' knowledge among consumers, who then rub workers in the food industry up the wrong way, as they seek to trade on that knowledge by criticizing any food served for them that does not match the airbrushed and photoshopped gastro-porn images of the food media (Fattorini, 1994). Consumers famously want – and often get – only sanitized product knowledge, purged of the (often grimy) realities of the production and distribution process (Cook and Crang, 1996). The city mapped by celebrity chefs on their sojourns book-signing tours, and the city mapped by the food miles many ingredients travel: here are two peculiar cartographies of eating today.

Eating 'other' spaces

Of course, the city is a map of culinary tastes and status-driven eating habits in countless other ways. Even its spatial layout reflects the dance of culinary-cultural capital, and the territorial forces of urban development are transformed into taste zones as surely as class maps the city's residential districts. So-called ethnic quarters exemplify this process. The settling of immigrant communities in cities has often resulted in the formation of clusters; ghettos and neighbourhoods, Little Italies and Chinatowns. These districts mark simultaneously the desire for familiarity in a strange city and the practices of exclusion that keep social groups confined. The balance between elected and enforced concentration is context-specific, and requires thick historical reading to unravel. One thing is clear: assimilation is not always desirable nor achievable (Young, 2000).

As a way of rebranding ghettos, the practice of designating urban quarters has become a prominent re-imaging strategy for cities (Jayne, 2000). Here we are concerned with so-called ethnic quarters, though we can see this process expanded to 'quarter' other social groups – in gay villages, for example – as well as production and consumption activities, as in jewellery quarters, cultural quarters, etc. (Bell and Jayne, 2003). What is the meaning and purpose of quartering? As I have already said, it is partly a spin on residential and commercial segregation. But it also makes over those districts, profiling their distinctiveness, and thereby ambivalently celebrating or commodifying them (Gorman, 2000). Quartering is, therefore, a kind of theming – a way of producing the urban landscape as a readerly text (Gottdeiner, 1997). The readers are visitors, of course. The imperative to quarter is economic as much as it is cultural: by cooking up ethnic quarters, we render them visible and accessible. To the communities that inhabit them, of course, no such visibilizing is necessary. This is making those districts available for consumption, as stages for the playing out of cultural omnivorousness:

> We spend a Sunday afternoon walking through Chinatown, or checking out this week's eccentric players in the park. We look at restaurants, stores, and clubs with something new for us, a new ethnic food, a different atmosphere, a different crowd of people. We walk through sections of the city that we experience as having unique characters which are not ours, where people from diverse places mingle and then go home. (Young, 1990, p. 239)

That's Iris Marion Young, cosmopolitan intellectual, enjoying the *frisson* of wandering out of her own neighbourhood, but not noticing that other people live there: 'people from diverse places mingle *and then go home*', leaving the people that live there to tidy up, ready for the next influx of culture-hungry omnivores. The Sunday stroll through Chinatown is here cast as the new-middle-class equivalent of the drive-through – a strategic strike that minimizes the uncomfortable contact of more sustained engagement. Ghassan Hage (1997) vividly describes these excursions of denial – denying the labour that produces the goods and places consumed. Jean Duruz (1999, 2000), however, cautions against oversimplifying things here, noting that relations between consumer and producer in these sites are complex. Reading ethnic quarters as either fabulous sites of multi-cultural difference or as spaces of continuing colonial fetishism and appropriation misses the intricacies of encounters that occur there. True, both those imperatives can be present, but the relative push and pull of each is unpredictable and subject to change. As with countless other 'encounters over the counter' in multi-cultural urban eating places, identities are produced and consumed in nuanced and contingent interactions (Ferraro, 2002; Parker, 2000).

Given the movement of cultural capital, socially and spatially, quarters are prone to fads and fashions that make them trendy one moment and *passé* the next. A British Sunday newspaper with an omnivorous readership recently ran a tour guide to the cuisines and foodstuffs of the UK's major 'ethnic groups'. It laid out for readers the way to negotiate 'ethnic supermarkets', telling us what to look for, and what to do with the ingredients we find there. That's the paradox of democratizing culinary-cultural capital, however – the paradox that cultures can suddenly be dumped, as the taste-makers notice the downward spiral of culinary-cultural capital. So this laying bare of the secrets of the Japanese supermarket marks the beginning of a process that can lead, in some cases, to the total *indigenization* of cuisines, such that they no longer confer any authentic ethnic 'exoticness'.

We can watch this process in action as individual foodstuffs migrate across the foodscape, from the 'obscurity' of ethnic foodstores to the deli counter, from there to the supermarkets' 'ethnic food' aisles, and then out into the collective shopping basket and belly. The migratory movement of something like olive oil in the UK tracks this democratization, ending with olive oil sitting on shelves shoulder-to-shoulder with other cooking oils, such as the lowly vegetable oil. While there might still be a cultural cachet attached to olive oil here – signified by its price, for one thing, as well as by its packaging – it has become emptied of much of its cultural signification. One no longer need venture to Little Italy to source it. Another Italian anecdote illustrates this point, too: Italian restaurants, newspapers tell us, are soon to be subject to authentication by Italian government reps, keen to maintain the quality of their food service by linking it back to the homeland. As a defensive response to the percolation of Italian cooking and eating out from Italy and all its global Little Italies, this initiative neatly highlights the democratization problem: once Italian food is so disembedded from its source, the culinary-cultural value attaching

Hospitality, Leisure & Tourism Series

to the signifier 'Italianness' begins to devalue, and thus needs some shoring-up through nationalist authentication. Eating Italian now comes with a guarantee, re-embedding it in its origin – or at least to its origin's outposts, the ethnic quarters. Again, this cements the connection between ethnic identity and food production, since only Italians can make quality-assured Italian food – but this can also mean the reverse, too: that Italians can make *only* Italian food.

If ethnic quarters are therefore (ambivalently) celebrated for mummifying immigrant cuisines in a protective coating of authenticity, making available a kind of cosmopolitan tourism-at-home, then they have to be read as one particular culinary-geographic strategy for making up the city-food equation. From another angle, nothing sums up the postmodern metropolis better than the frantic commingling of cultures and cuisines – making fusion food a culinary cypher for *multi-culti/cosmo-metro* life. Instead of preserving distinct ethnic cultures, they are here mixed, or rather *allowed to collide*: not blended in some melting pot out of which comes an indistinct melange, but cultures rubbing up against each other, jostling, making new and surprising juxtapositions. Syncretic combinations emerge that hybridize and creolize diverse ingredients, playfully pick-and-mixing (James, 1996). Here's Elizabeth Miles on one US star of fusion food: 'Wolfgang Puck creates cuisine that both expresses his own identity(ies), and mirrors what he perceives as the identity(ies) of his customers ... [T]hese identities reflect the multi-ethnic, multi-cultural, multi-gendered, nomadic paradigms of postmodernism' (Miles, 1993, p. 193) – the dishes articulate 'points of identification' (p. 195), complexly and playfully combining ingredients and cooking practices: 'No "real" nor "intended" meaning emerges from this accretion of foods, vocabularies and techniques, but rather a pastiche of possible readings' (p. 196). Like the postmodern architecture of many metropolitan centres, subject of endless urban theorizing, Puck's equally postmodern food plays with consumers' expectations, flattering them for their sophisticated deconstructive eating habits.

Of course, for some folk it is not very far from fusion to *con-fusion*, and reactions to fusion food can play up the boundary-blurring dangers of over-fusioning – again mirroring writing on urban postmodernism (e.g. Jameson, 1991). This is often disguised as a clash of tastes, but can be read as distaste about the clash of cultures, too. Against this, the purity and authenticity of distinct cuisines practices a subtle but nonetheless insidious form of ethnic (palate) cleansing. Eating 'foreign' food is okay, so long as the borders are not breached; culinary miscegenation threatens confusion in the same way as other multiculturalist moments. Moreover, the jump from fusion to confusion invokes the con-trick: the suspicion that repackaging cuisines in this way is some kind of sleight-of-hand, some act of dishonesty. Fusion is in this reading a weak or lazy way of conferring one's own multi-culti sensibility: safer to be in Spago than trying to enact creolization in other spheres of life (Ferraro, 2002; Hage, 1997).

Miles includes another useful dimension in her reading of Puck: that his dishes also speak of the relationship between the city and nature: 'These recipes presume a great, diverse natural bounty magically melting from specific farmland and ocean locations into the decentered city. This is the postmodern landscape, where nature meets city in a seamless continuum of goods and commodities' (Miles, 1993, p. 199). Abundance and availability are here factored in, domesticating nature by cooking and eating it. The city is the stage for this process: the place where nature turns into culture and nurture. The farmers' market can here be figured as the flipside of (con)fusion food – in the space of the farmers' market, the country visits the city and offers itself up. Integrity, honesty, simplicity – the market offers a postmodern version of premodern eating, remaking formerly peasant food as the new feast of kings.

The case of fish and chips in the UK serves as a final illustration. Dethroned from mass tastes by the new dominance of US-imported coffee shops, fish and chips now appear gentrified, on the menus of slick seafood eateries, with a price tag to match (on the history of fish and chips in Britain, see Walton, 1992). If a New Labour politician famously once embarrassed himself by confusing the mushy peas on offer at a chippy with guacamole, confirming (so the press said) his lack of contact with the 'common people', it now seems he's more likely to be acquainting himself with 'pea guacamole' on his high-priced chip supper while his constituents nibble on an avocado-on-rye deli sandwich accompanied by a decaff latte. Such is the turnover in positional goods and cultural capital – a turnover reflected in the streetscape, as chippies close and Starbucks open another franchise.

Conclusion

These cityscapes of eating out can be read as maps of broader urban social processes: trends in food consumption, such as the popularity of 'ethnic' eating or the taste for fusion foods, both reflect and are reflective of those broader processes. Cities are dynamic things, and so are tastes. The ebb and flow of capital, the impact of gentrification, attempts to rebrand cities, the temporary and permanent movement of people between and within cities – these processes can be traced through the eating-out habits of urban dwellers and urban visitors. Whether attempting to fix taste in 'fortress cuisines' (Duruz, 2000) or mix taste in postmodern *bricolage*, these food fashions are played out spatially: new districts become trendy, fast food joints get clustered on peripheral sites, Turkish kebab vendors in Germany become Italian restaurateurs to keep pace with taste trends (Calgar, 1995). Just as classical urban theory sees capital as the motor of urban transformation, so we can hear see *cultural* capital driving change in cityscapes. The cultural intermediaries – like the urban pioneers associated with gentrification (Smith and Williams, 1986) – have as important a role to play as urban planners, estate agents and architects. For in defining taste, and identifying its spaces within the city, they are actively remoulding the neighbourhoods and districts that come in to and fall out of fashion. Recent interest in the so-called creative class (Florida, 2002) reveals the increasing awareness of the role of cultural intermediaries in changing urban fortunes: footloose capital and cultural capital are here channelled in the same direction, and it is not stretching a point to suggest that indices of 'culinary diversity' have a part to play in locational decisions among this group.

In this chapter, then, I have attempted to suggest some of the logics at work in the spaces of contemporary Western urban eating out. Maps of restaurant locations tell us much more than stories of the land market or of happenstance: they reflect the territorialized taste cultures of interest groups with forms of power (especially cultural capital). Today, perhaps more than ever, the new middle class (or creative class) is at the heart of this process, in making and placing taste hierarchies. These hierarchies are both economic and cultural – just as neighbourhoods within cities witness changing fortunes as they feel (or are sidestepped by) the forces of gentrification and urban renewal, so individual eateries, types of eatery, and areas associated with different kinds of eating are also shaped and reshaped by the forces of culinary gentrification and gustatory renewal. As I said at the outset, eating out is thus a concentration of much broader processes working at a whole set of different spatial scales: at the scale of the plate or the dining table, their power is no less acutely felt.

Notes

Some of these ideas were first worked through, somewhat sketchily, in 'All you can eat: fragmente fur eine neue urbane kulinarische geographie', in Regina Bittner (ed) *Urbane Paradiese: zur kulturgeschichte modernen vergnugens*, 2001, Frankfurt/ New York: Bauhaus/Campus.

Bibliography

Appadurai, Arjun (1990). Disjuncture and difference in the global cultural economy. In *Global Culture: Nationalism, Globalization and Modernity* (Mike Featherstone, Ed.). London: Sage Publications, pp. 295–310.

Bell, David and Jayne, Mark (Eds) (2003). *City of Quarters*. Aldershot: Ashgate.

Bourdieu, Pierre (1984). *Distinction: A Social Critique of the Judgement of Taste*. London: Routledge.

Calgar, Ayse (1995). McDoner: Doner kebab and the social positioning struggle of German Turks. In *Marketing in a Multicultural World* (Janeen Costa and Gary Bamossy, Eds). London: Sage Publications, pp. 209–230.

Cook, Ian and Crang, Phil (1996). The world on a plate: culinary culture, displacement and geographical knowledge. *Journal of Material Culture* **1**, 131–153.

Dekkers, Midas (2000). *The Way of All Flesh: The Romance of Ruins*. New York: FSG.

Hospitality, Leisure & Tourism Series

Duruz, Jean (1999). The streets of Clovelly: food, difference and place-making. *Continuum: Journal of Media and Cultural Studies* **13**, 305–314.

Duruz, Jean (2000). A nice baked dinner … or two roast ducks from Chinatown? identity grazing. *Continuum: Journal of Media and Cultural Studies* **14**, 289–301.

Fattorini, Joseph (1994). Food journalism: a medium for conflict? *British Food Journal* **96** (10), 24–28.

Ferraro, Sylvia (2002). *Comida isn par*. Consumption of Mexican food in Los Angeles: "foodscapes" in a transnational consumer society. In *Food Nations: Selling Taste in Consumer Societies* (Warren Belasco and Philip Scranton, Eds). London: Routledge, pp. 194–219.

Finkelstein, Joanne (1998). Dining out: the hyperreality of appetite. In *Eating Culture* (Ron Scapp and Brian Seitz, Eds). Albany: SUNY Press, pp. 201–215.

Florida, Richard (2002). *The Rise of the Creative Class*. New York: Basic Books.

French, Sean (1995). First catch your puffin. *Granta* **52**, 197–202.

Gorman, Tony (2000). Otherness and citizenship: towards a politics of the plural community. In *City Visions* (David Bell and Azzedine Haddour, Eds). Harlow: Prentice Hall, pp. 219–232.

Gottdeiner, Mark (1997). *The Theming in America: Dreams, Visions, and Commercial Spaces*. Boulder CO: Westview.

Hage, Ghassan (1997). At home in the entrails of the west: multiculturalism, ethnic food and migrant home-building. In *Home/World: Space, Community and Marginality in Sydney's West* (Helen Grace, Ghassan Hage, Lesley Johnson, Julie Langworth and Michael Symonds, Eds). Annandale: Pluto, pp. 99–153.

Hannerz, Ulf (1990). Cosmopolitans and locals in world culture. In *Global Culture: Nationalism, Globalization and Modernity* (Mike Featherstone, Ed.). London: Sage Publications, pp. 237–252.

Holloway, Lewis and Kneafsey, Moya (2000). Reading the space of the farmers' market: a preliminary investigation from the UK. *Sociologica Ruralis*, **40** (3), 285–299.

James, Allison (1996). Cooking the books: global or local identities in contemporary British food cultures? In *Cross-Cultural*

Consumption: Global Markets, Local Realities (David Howes, Ed.). London: Routledge, pp. 77–92.

Jameson, Fredric (1991). *Postmodernism, or, the Cultural Logic of Late Capitalism*. London: Verso.

Jayne, Mark (2000). Imag(in)ing a post-industrial Potteries. In *City Visions* (David Bell and Azzedine Haddour, Eds). Harlow: Prentice Hall, pp. 12–26.

Miles, Elizabeth (1993). Adventures in the postmodernist kitchen: the cuisine of Wolfgang Puck. *Journal of Popular Culture*, **27**, 191–203.

O'Neill, John (1999). Have you had your theory today? In *Resisting McDonaldization* (Barry Smart, Ed.). London: Sage Publications, pp. 41–56.

Parker, David (2000). The Chinese takeaway and the diasporic habitus: space, time and power geometries. In *Un/Settled Multiculturalisms: Diasporas, Entanglements, Transruptions* (Barnor Hesse, Ed.). London: Zed Books, pp. 73–95.

Puck, Wolfgang (1996). Untitled interview. *Aperture* **143**, 63.

Ritzer, George (1993). *The McDonaldization of Society*. London: Sage Publications.

Smith, Neil and Williams, Peter (Eds) (1986). *Gentrification of the City*. London: Allen & Unwin.

Walton, John R. (1992). *Fish & Chips and the British Working Class, 1870–1940*. Leicester: Leicester University Press.

Warde, Alan and Martens, Lydia (1998). The prawn cocktail ritual. In *Consuming Passions: Food in the Age of Anxiety* (Sian Griffiths and Jennifer Wallace, Eds). London: Mandolin, pp. 118–122.

Warde, Alan and Martens, Lydia (2000). *Eating Out: Social Differentiation, Consumption and Pleasure*. Cambridge: Cambridge University Press.

Warde, Alan, Martens, Lydia and Olsen, Wendy (1999). Consumption and the problem of variety: cultural omnivorousness, social distinction and dining out. *Sociology* **33**, 105–127.

Young, Iris Marion (1990). *Justice and the Politics of Difference*. Princeton: Princeton University Press.

Young, Iris Marion (2000). A critique of integration as the remedy for segregation, In *City Visions* (David Bell and Azzedine Haddour, Eds). Harlow: Prentice Hall, pp. 205–218.

Zukin, Sharon (1995). *The Cultures of Cities*. Oxford: Blackwell.

Hospitality, Leisure & Tourism Series

4

Chic cuisine: the impact of fashion on food

Joanne Finkelstein

The consumption of food, like the satisfying of any appetite, has long since ceased to be about nutrition and has come instead to contain myriad social, cultural and symbolic meanings. In the consumer dominated societies of the industrialized era, every conceivable human idea, cultural practice and material substance seems to have been transformed by 'market forces' into desirable commodities to be pursued and possessed. The consumer society puts everything up for sale and food has been no exception. This makes the desire for food not a simple matter of meeting basic nutritional needs, but part of a social discourse in which personal and collective identities are defined and presented. Food has thus been thoroughly transformed into symbol, icon, trope, sign and status.

For example, Bell and Valentine (1997, pp. 1–2) open their book on the geography of food with dialogue from the screenplay of Quentin Tarantino's innovative film, Pulp Fiction. The scene is of two murderous criminals driving in the streets of Hollywood, California and idly chatting. One has recently returned from Europe and is reporting on the quaint food tastes of the French who transform the McDonald's quarter-pounder with cheese into the exotic sounding royale with cheese and the Dutch who serve french fries with mayonnaise instead of ketchup.

The scene is humorous on various levels, but its apposite-ness here is as an illustration of how common it is to find the topic of food a focus for popular culture. Food has become a source of entertainment; indeed, it could be argued that from the beginnings of the European restaurant in the seventeenth century, food has always been more about entertainment and fashion than about sustenance.

Toying with food

That food is not food anymore can be seen from its transform-ation into various and sometimes frivolous amusements such as the Fabergé egg, bananas in Pyjamas, chocolate novelty golfballs, cigarettes, animals, stiletto-heeled shoes and mobile phones. The use of food in a non-edible capacity is not new. Australians are familiar with the actor Barry Humphries as the alter ego of Dame Edna Everidge, the strident housewife from Moonee Ponds who has socially climbed further than most people can imagine. But in the late 1950s, Humphries was a multi-media artist of a different kind, creating objects from unusual materials. One such piece was a highly coloured can-vas made from baked cake. It used lamingtons, fruit cake, sponge fingers, rainbow tiara cake, swiss roll, fairy cake and sprinkles of hundreds-n-thousands (tiny fragments of coloured sugar), crafted into a wall-mounted landscape called *cakescape*. This highly textured piece was both a parody of the Australian fascination with landscape paintings and an ingenious crafting of an art form using banal materials.

Playing with food has a long history. The great French chef Antonin Carême (1784–1833) established architectural food as part of his Grande Cuisine. As amusing additions to the meal, he constructed inedible pieces montées with Italian, Turkish, Russian, Chinese, Egyptian and Gallic themes. In a contempor-ary setting, the Japanese artist, Ryoichi Majima has incorporated food into sculptural installations as a means of commenting on and critiquing its role in society. In 1995, Majima completed Noodle Boy and Noodle Girl, two separate works which comment savagely on the relationship between food, power and pleasure. Each sculpture consists of a round ceramic rice bowl, about 1.5 m in diameter, which resembles those commonly found in inexpensive Asian restaurants. Noodle Boy is immersed in the bowl, with only his head and shoulders visible above a soup containing large pieces of floating spring onion, bamboo shoots, water chestnuts, bacon and noodles. There is a television floating in the bowl as well, and Noodle Boy, with his mouth stuffed with long strands of noodle and two chopsticks, seems to be watching the television screen. In situ, the TV monitor is hooked into a closed circuit which shows both the gallery space in which the sculpture is being displayed and the spectators as they walk around the piece. The Noodle Boy, sitting in the soup, is a young man about to take his place in society. He has a wide-eyed expression, a trimmed, bleached yellow Mohawk haircut. Any expectations of a bright future ahead of him are undercut by his present situation. He is naked (or appears to be); the tendons in his neck are strained as his mouth is forced wide open to accept an overload of food. The aura of the piece is dark; Noodle Boy himself appears to be a kind of fodder. The complementary piece, Noodle Girl, also gestures towards an alarming future. The Noodle Girl is also sitting in a large bowl filled with soup and floating vegetable matter. Again, there is a television screen, propped between her raised, spread legs. She is positioned for a gynaecological examination. She seems vulnerable; her head is tilted back, her mouth stuffed with noodles and an oversized pair of chopsticks, held by a huge invisible hand, is forcing food down her throat. Her feet, with bright red painted toe-nails, are propped up on the rim of the bowl, astride the TV monitor.

Majima's sculptures comment on the epicurism that dominates the modern food market. Noodle Boy and Noodle Girl along with his many other food installations provide a commentary on our desire for food, on fashionable tastes and the exaggerated interest we appear to have in food. The foodstuffs we encounter in fast-food outlets, elegant department stores, on grocery shelves, in galleries and art exhibitions, at street stalls and so on, are loquacious objects. Situating food as the subject of so much commentary draws attention to the fashionable and appetitive cycles that direct our tastes. The early nineteenth century food philosopher Jean Anthelme Brillat-Savarin offered the now famous aphorism, we are what we eat, which suggested, among other ideas that the plasticity of food and our enthusiasm for toying with it is a fundamental element of human society.

Social role of food

Irrespective of a society's economic organization as agrarian, feudal, capitalist or communal, food is always part of an elaborate symbol system that conveys cultural messages. Mundane personal attributes such as status, gender, age, sexuality and ethnic identity become visible in the food that is selected and served. Food is also capable of representing ephemeral personal qualities such as élan and sangfroid. Tastes for specialized items such as squid, squab pigeon, oysters, raw tuna and offal speak of such claims. In various ways, food is deeply associative; Peter Mayle's (1991) best selling travel novel offers the local cuisine to the reader as part of the process of self-discovery; Alphonso Lingis (1994) provides a philosophy of appetite that includes an explanation of such exotic habits as that of the Incas who dined alone with a spread of gold and jewelled utensils; Freud (1900) has provided a memorable interpretation of a dream about smoked salmon that is less about food and more about sexual anxiety and social respectability. Mary Douglas (1970) has developed taxonomy of foods based on whether they are pure and edible or unclean and polluting. This classification is not just about specific cultural knowledge, it is as well a theory of human subjectivity. She presents an argument that explains why individuals cannot afford to consume 'unclean' foods or cross cultural barriers by tasting novelties, because in so doing they incorporate the 'foreign' into the human body and are thereby exposed to attacks on their vital essence. Accordingly, Douglas (1979) deciphers a meal in terms of idiosyncratic cultural practices as well as a cosmology of subjectivity. Food has the capacity to encapsulate a variety of meanings that extend its social value beyond the obvious.

Hospitality, Leisure & Tourism Series

Food can be thought of as both an empty and over-determined signifier which functions as a text through which much of modern social life becomes intelligible. For instance, where and what we eat, with whom, at what time of day or night, are directly influenced by a variety of everyday factors such as age, gender, social status and income. Bell and Valentine (1997, p. 3) have noted that 'every mouthful, every meal, can tell us something about ourselves, and about our place in the world'. Food is at once universal and mundane, yet vividly revealing of specific cultural habits.

In every society, the nature of food and its distribution are directly influenced by a range of seemingly remote economic, technological, political, cultural, historical and sociological factors. In the consumer society, these influences arise from a variety of sources; for example, the mass production of the motor car, the development of the supermarket, the arrival of television and commercial advertising, factory farming techniques and so on. Each of these, and many others, have been significant in shaping patterns of food consumption and creating the general view that food is a modern amusement and part of contemporary popular culture. Of further influence has been the popularity of the restaurant and the rise of the hospitality industries and tourism. The architecture of modern cities also contributes in so far as most major cities boast a huge variety of cuisines which sometimes give name to specific neighbourhoods such as 'little Italy', 'Chinatown', 'the French Quarter' and 'the (fast food) strip'. These fashions in food have a further influence on satellite industries such as television cookery programs, new styles of food packaging, the publication of cook books, the growth in boutique vineyards and so on. As part of the tourism and hospitality industries, food has become a site of multifarious entertainments shaped in large part by culinary internationalism and cultural migration. It is the very ordinariness of food itself that has enabled it to be written over by a multitude of cultural practices and values.

In the industrialized societies where consumption of goods and experiences is taken for granted, food has been altered from an appetite to a form of renewable desire. It has been long divorced from its function as a source of nutrition and redefined as a source of innovative pleasure. Marion Nestle (2002, p. 5)

Hospitality, Leisure & Tourism Series

tells us that 'people throughout the world eat many different foods and follow many different dietary patterns...' This diversity supports the idea that food is highly distinctive yet characteristic.

Shifts in contemporary tastes are frequently linked to marketing cycles which are further connected to supply chains in related industries where there are influential technological innovations in manufacture and distribution. Developing tastes for certain products is part of food marketing. Nestle (2002, p. 1) has pointed out that on a global scale, 'food companies must convince people to eat more of their products...' They are active in developing fads and fashions in consumer tastes in order to promote their business. While the popularity of snack foods may appear directly connected to changed methods in advertising such as product placement in films, music video clips and so on, other conditions such as agricultural practices and technological advances in manufacture are also part of creating novel taste habits. The popularity of food items such as sweetened drinks, ice cream, baked biscuits, pre-prepared and frozen meals, are all part of a process that attempts to cultivate and control certain desires for food. In no small part, the restaurant has played a primary role in the processes that change and cultivate new food desires, and as such, it can be thought of as a social laboratory with the capacity to commodify foods and change consumer tastes.

The importance of the restaurant

The term 'restaurant' takes on its modern form in the nineteenth century as a place where meals can be purchased at various times of the day and night. The original meaning of the word refers specifically to a French health fashion to imbibe a medicinal soup, consommé or nourishing juice, prepared for sickly individuals (see Furetière, *Dictionnaire Universel*, 1708). The transformation of the term *restaurant* from its eighteenth century original meaning as a restorative bouillon to its current meaning as a fashionable and convenient place to eat and drink has become a fertile area of scholarship in cultural theory and history principally because it parallels and encapsulates much of the modernizing experience that characterizes western society.[1]

Hospitality, Leisure & Tourism Series

The idea of the restaurant (as a place of nourishment) begins in different forms in different locations without an agreed or necessary originary point. The restaurant and its antecedents can be linked to the 'cook shops' of the medieval city which prepared foods for those without home cooking facilities, which was most people. It is associated with the seventeenth century coffee houses that arose in London as purveyors of coffee and tobacco which also provided a vibrant meeting place for the exchange of information about business activities in the city, parliament and at the docks. In various parts of Europe and Asia, elements of the modern restaurant were to be found in markets, bazaars, travellers' inns, village kitchens, wineshops and taverns. All of which were rudimentary restaurants insofar as they met the appetitive needs of paying customers.

From its modern origins in a small cup of bouillon, the restaurant has been recognized as part of the complex transformations that have produced the contemporary liberal era. The restaurant has been associated with changes in sensibilities and pleasures; it has been seen as influential in the democratization of luxury and the dissemination of fashionability; it has functioned as both a symbol of civility and a mechanism for spreading the civilizing process (Elias, 1978). When the restaurant became a place where women and men could display themselves in public, it was immediately important as a site where experimental styles of human exchange and play were negotiated and practised. The restaurant made evident the complex interdependencies between individuals and their socio-economic circumstances, and in these ways became the background against which individuals learned to disport themselves and dissemble, to gain social advantage. This atmosphere constructed the restaurant as a form of spectacle in which the objects on display included both people and foodstuffs. The restaurant contributed to the visibility of self-identity and to the creation of celebrity by being a site where the famous could be seen by the not famous, and where celebrity chefs and restaurateurs could make their reputations.[2] In short, the modern restaurant was (and remains) an eloquent signifier of sociability and a mechanism for status competition and fashionability.

From its earliest incarnation, the restaurant has been intricately involved with various social influences and in particular

Hospitality, Leisure & Tourism Series

with the emergence of modern fashion. Despite appearances, the restaurant was not simply a commercial enterprise where goods and services were systematically exchanged; it was always a crucible in which a variety of appetites and desires were cultivated, and where the processes of generating new social experiences were constantly being manufactured. Food is about sustenance and appetite, both physical and symbolic, and the distribution of food is about the organization of a society and the display of status and power. Thus, to take note of who eats what with whom and where, is to cast light on a host of political, economic and cultural practices. As Terry Eagleton (1998, p. 204) has summarized, food is 'endlessly interpretable, as gift, threat, poison, recompense, barter, seduction, solidarity, suffocation'. However, it is not as much the plasticity of foodstuffs that explains the social value of the restaurant as it is the variety of human activities that have come to circulate around food and which have made the restaurant more than its origins ever suggested.

The restaurant à la mode

Nineteenth century Paris has been described as having a restaurant on every corner. They provided for every conceivable taste and became the well-recognized icons of the city. These bustling eating and drinking establishments, incorporating many of the habits of the earlier seventeenth and eighteenth century coffee houses, played a significant part in shaping the character of the modern era by bringing people together from various social strata in an unregulated mix that created opportunities for new ideas, tastes and values. In this way, they acted as a social barometer, sensitively recording and nurturing the various influences and undercurrents that were invisibly creating the fabric of the future society. Rebecca Spang has argued that much of the importance of the restaurant lies with its contribution to modern cosmopolitanism. Diners in the restaurant were making history by producing new forms of sociality: 'to be conversant with the protocols, rituals, and vocabulary of restaurant going was to be quintessentially Parisian and supremely sophisticated' (Spang, 2000, p. 172).

Of its various functions, the role of the restaurant in the shaping of modern social manners is perhaps most interesting.

From its beginnings, it was a site where the individual's repertoire of claims for identity and social status could be tested and displayed. For men initially and then for women, it provided a stage setting where techniques of sociability could be developed and demonstrated. The restaurant itself contributed to this dramaturgy by augmenting the individual's social presence in much the same way that the domestic sphere came to extend and make visible the sensibilities of the nineteenth century bourgeois woman (Felski, 1995). The restaurant was (and remains) a structuring element in the long-term experimentation with social relations that underpin modern, mercantile society.

Sennett (1994, p. 345) has given an interesting account of how the restaurant was directly responsible for creating certain manners of decorum and rules of sociability. He gives the example of the eighteenth century English coffee house which encouraged, for the first time, the intermingling of different classes of men (not women) all motivated by interests in public news and gossip about business, trade opportunities and local power alliances. From this swill of talk, the benefits of crossing class barriers in a public meeting place were quickly learned. In the cafés of Paris of the ancient regime, and prior to the dramatic events of the French Revolution, political groups were able to congregate. The café provided a safe public space from which to recruit members and generate solidarity through open discussion. The café provided a new domain where strangers intermingled, and where for the price of a drink, any individual was physically positioned in close enough proximity with others and could thus initiate a conversation with whomever they chose. Providing this democratic space where great varieties of people literally brushed up against one another proved to be an important factor in the fashioning of the modern manners required for metropolitan life. Most obviously, the café society required the individual to develop a greater sense of trust and acceptance of the stranger who seemed always to be standing nearby.

Fashioning the modern restaurant

From these experimental spaces in sociability, new styles of restaurants quickly developed. The small street cafés, or cafés intimes, had become immediately popular as meeting places for those aspirants who required a sequestered space to plot political activities and hatch out schemes for transforming society. In a short space of time, these dark corners gave way to cafés with tables and chairs placed outdoors, in full view of the grand boulevards of Paris. This relocation to a different streetscape destroyed the privacy needed by the revolutionary, and replaced it with a larger and more theatrical setting, where passers-by could watch those seated at tables as if they were on a stage, and in turn they themselves could be watched by strollers-by. This change in spatial arrangements had an immediate effect on the style of sociality in the restaurant. The outdoor café required people to stay seated at the one table, unlike the sequestered coffee house where individuals moved freely from group to group, or one argumentative cluster to another. The outdoor café appealed to a different clientele – the middle and upper classes. These larger cafés provided slower waiter service in comparison to the speedy bar service of the bustling coffee house and became, instead, a quiet resting place where individuals could sit in public undisturbed, for lengthy periods of time and yet still be entertained. Sennett (1994, p. 346) quotes nineteenth century traveller Augustus Hare on the charms of the café terrace, separated from the bustle of street life: 'Half an hour spent on the boulevards or on one of the chairs in the Tuileries gardens has the effect of an infinitely diverting theatrical performance'.

The significance of these different styles of restaurant and café demonstrates how new sensibilities and pleasures were being cultivated in individuals. The restaurant was the site where novel forms of association were being enjoyed and where the situational tensions between spatiality and sociality were being mediated. The nineteenth century sociologist, Georg Simmel (1950) observed, in his prescient analyses of modern metropolitan life, that the physical proximity of strangers in places like restaurants, public parks, railway carriages and theatres, created the circumstances in which individuals developed new ways of thinking and seeing as well as new emotions and manners of behaving. Simmel made a point of comparing the theatre and railway carriage as sites where the architecture shaped the interior sensations. Both these places required people to sit together in silence, for long periods of time, often with little else to do but stare ahead, into open space. Sitting in public in this way was a new experience. The modern railway carriages arranged their seating with everyone facing forward, unlike the previous mode of transport, the horse-drawn carriage, which positioned individuals opposite one another. Simmel theorized that the advent of mass transport, along with mass entertainment in theatres, parks, cafés and so on, proved to be the material circumstances that created the blasé attitude. For Simmel, metropolitan life trained individuals in the blunting of affect; it required them not to respond to others or acknowledge their circumstances, but to appear bland even oblivious at all times. This mien was a form of protection from the raucous intrusion of ungoverned street life. The blasé attitude blunted the unwanted assaults or demands from the noisy, visually stimulating street life of the city; it cultivated that particular capacity, so common in the modern world of the twentieth and twenty-first centuries, of being surrounded by life but remaining detached from it.

The popularity of the modern restaurant has depended precisely upon the cultivation of this new psychological reserve which allowed individuals to enjoy the entertainment of being in public and come under the scrutinizing gaze of the stranger but, at the same time, feel unthreatened as if they were merely another element in the broad panorama of the spectacle itself. The diner enjoys the entertainment and is also part of the entertainment itself. Throughout the twentieth and into the twenty-first century, the numbers and varieties of restaurants in the metropolitan centres of the industrializing world have continued to grow in popularity and social utility, and have continued as well to contribute to contemporary cosmopolitanism.[3] As Spang (2000) noted for the eighteenth century, a city's restaurants measured its vibrancy and sophistication. The areas of a city where restaurants concentrated, such as the Palais-Royal and Latin Quarter in Paris and Covent Garden in London, have become fashionable locations. Travel guides from the nineteenth century onwards commonly referred to restaurants as part of the local colour. Restaurants had become the trope through which to understand the distinctiveness of particular ways of life.

A century or more later, the restaurant has assumed multifarious forms. It is now part of a global multi-billion dollar industry, a tourist attraction, luxury entertainment and social convenience. It has extended beyond its early functions as a crucible for the revolutionary, innovatory and recreational, to become, in the twentieth century, part of the industrialized society's large scale economic structure and international position. Yet the restaurant retains a human scale insofar as it is often used by the individual as a personal totem to indicate private values. For example, a favourite vegan restaurant might reflect an individual's personal attitudes toward health and the environment. It might represent the diner's strong attitudes to food including the ethical concerns around animal farming and livestock for food. It might also suggest a concern with genetic modification of grains, vegetarianism, organic foods, health foods, laboratory manufacture of smart foods, nutriceuticals and so on. In short, the attractions and pleasures of the restaurant and the cultural habits around dining out can transform the diner into a stakeholder who oftentimes takes a strong interest in the complex public discourses on the morality and fashionability of different food styles and practices.

In these various guises, Spang (2000, p. 3) has argued the restaurant is and has always been the site for complicated histories of numerous social, economic and political innovations. Its own history of evolution from a small cup of soup to a political and social crucible of radical thought and then to a diversionary refuge and haven closely allied with the entertainment industries, mirrors many of the complex changes that have shaped industrialized societies over the past 200 years.

Consumer fashions

The restaurant does not have a singular character yet it is a popular site for the satisfaction of various appetites. In this sense, its most basic function, that of delivering food at the request of a paying customer, provides a minimal definition. Now, in its myriad forms, it houses new political activities including postcolonial claims of identity, innovative medical regimes and health fads, and experimental social engagements that cross the divides of class and gender. Its proliferation has not obeyed definable and orderly principles; its success is tied to the explosion in human tastes and social activities that characterize the modern, liberal era.[4]

The similarities and differences between restaurants as diverse as the McDonald's fast food outlet, Terence Conran's massive *Mezzo* with its 700 tables, *Windows on the World* at the 107th level of New York's now vaporized World Trade Center and the legendary *Tour d'argent*, are useful devices to focus attention on the complex social relations that occur in that particular sector of the modern public domain.

Much of the driving force beneath the proliferation of the restaurant is related to the expansion of the consumer economy. As Marion Nestle (2002, p. 300) has noted of the food industries in general, '... new products [are] the key to expanding sales ...'. The earliest restaurateurs understood this modern economic principle. César Ritz, who opened the opulent dining room at London's Savoy Hotel in 1889 knew that his bourgeois patrons were most interested in the theatricality of the restaurant, and especially the opportunities it offered to disport themselves, to play act, dissemble and to occupy the extravagant and opulent settings of the dining room as if it were their own.

As restaurateurs have long known, a smart decor can give a decisive edge over the competition. This knowledge underscored César Ritz's stylization of the grand dining room at the Savoy as a promenade for the bourgeoisie. Other restaurateurs have employed various gimmicks to enhance the drama of dining out, giving their establishments names that are meaningless but arresting (*The Quilted Giraffe, Liquidity, Planet Hollywood*) or offering distinctive styles of cuisine, and remarkable uniformed apparel for the staff. They have used the location of the kitchen, size of the wine glasses, design of the crockery, colour of the décor and cost of service as gimmicks and affectations that can distract the diner from the quality of the food: as the nineteenth century chef Antonin Carême knew well. He popularized the gimmick of food sculptures for precisely this reason. He made ornamental sculptures from spun sugar which could stand 4 and 5 feet in height and were shaped into bucolic scenes that included exotic pagodas, fountains and elaborate temples with cherubs adorning every possible nook and cranny. The purpose

Hospitality, Leisure & Tourism Series

of these confectionaries was to make the expense of dining out more akin to the purchase of a nebulous marvel, an experience that exulted the individual above others. It was, in short, conspicuous consumption as a claim for social superiority.

The early nineteenth-century commentator Jean Anthelme Brillat-Savarin (1825/1970) regarded restaurants as tableaux of bourgeois life. He claimed that one could always find in them an array of interesting characters: the lone male diner who orders his food in a loud voice, waits impatiently and eats quickly; families who delight in being out of the home; married couples who do not have much to say to one another but are quietly engrossed in watching the scene about them, and lovers who relish the constraints placed upon their ardour by being in public. He saw in restaurants the diners who acted as if they were regulars, who engaged the waiters with ostentatious familiarity, and the tourists who knew they would never return and so exploited their anonymity by unselfconsciously over-indulging. A hundred and fifty years after Brillat-Savarin, the restaurant is still a theatre, a scene worth observing, a public place full of possibilities but one which is at the same time familiar, reassuring and reliable (Finkelstein, 1989).

Restaurant architecture

A restaurant's décor and ambience symbolize the dining experience. Certain elements in the architecture of the restaurant convey information about what is being offered – the style of furniture, napery, lighting, floor covering, dress codes and so on, convey messages about luxury taste and the authenticity of the dining experience. Sometimes these codes are undercut by the exercise of fashion. For example, drinking a good wine can be made more difficult and hence less pleasurable if served in awkwardly shaped or out-sized glasses. Eating from a larger platter can be a source of irritation if the dining table is too small and the plate repeatedly clunks against crockery. The comfort of the seating, the level of lighting and noise, the colours and texture of the walls and ceiling are elements of dining that directly impinge on the diner's pleasure. These physical elements have little to do with the menu and comestibles themselves yet they exert a noticeable affect. In this way, the fashions in restaurant décor, cuisine and house style, all constitute important aspects of the dining experience.

Indeed, there is hardly an element in the dining experience that resists the influence of fashion. How the waiter behaves, his or her physical appearance and demeanour, the architecture of the restaurant, type of cuisine, hours of operation, size of the dining table, the location of the kitchen, the backstage services such as toilets, coat room, food storage system, are all subject to the vagaries of fashion. The restaurant is crowded with eloquent signifiers that shape the diner's pleasure, and all restaurants, whether they are the spectacular tourist attractions celebrated the world over or the local family bistro at the heart of a suburban community, are in the business of creating a particular atmosphere that is controlled through its immediate physical environment. The success or otherwise of these efforts is an intrinsic part of the fashionability and theatricality of dining out.

There are places to eat where the setting is much more important than the food. *The Four Seasons* in New York is celebrated for its décor, its famous art works, marble fish pond, gigantic chandelier, heavy silver service, and the menu which changes seasonally. The restaurant has been part of New York's cultural scene for years, not only as a trendsetter with cuisine and service but with its exclusive monthly wine tastings that bring together a select grouping of that city's elite (Trillin, 2002, p. 145). There are other restaurants which trade on their spectacular physical locations such as *La Tour D'Argent* overlooking the Seine in Paris, which also boasts being the original modern restaurant; *The Village Green* in New York with its English gardens, and *Bilson's* on Sydney's Circular Quay.

Conclusion

In a sense, the restaurant is a forerunner of the contemporary entertainment industry, which is in the business of marketing desires and constructing appetites. During its history it has enticed the social classes to imitate one another, it has been the arena in which class divisions have been safely breached, and where diverse human exchanges such as business deals,

Hospitality, Leisure & Tourism Series

seductions, family quarrels, etc. have taken place. It is where displays of social pretension, guile and the dictates of fashion have all been in evidence. The diner can pretend to be rich, urbane and powerful. S/he can play the role of gastronome, bon vivant, good father, benevolent mother, ardent lover and so on without any fear that the subterfuge will be exposed. In these many ways, the restaurant keeps abreast of shifting styles in tastes and behaviour, at the same time that it also fashions desires for many more pleasures than the prepared comestibles.

End notes

1 In Paris, in 1782, a take-out shopkeeper named Beauvilliers is credited with the establishment of the first in-principle restaurant. That is, he included in his shop, La grande Taverne de Londres, a number of small tables and chairs and served customers with a variety of dishes cooked on the premises. By serving these foods on the premises, Beauvilliers was functioning as a restaurateur and thus can be credited with the original concept. However, these originary moments evolve from a variety of preceding circumstances. Two decades before, in Paris, a soup vendor named Boulanger provided a place for the consumption of his restoratives (the original meaning of the term restaurant). In the 1760s, in New York, Samuel Fraunces opened a public house in lower Manhattan (not yet so named) where he sold beer and food, and hence, could be regarded as a restaurateur. In the 1680s, in London, there were the very popular coffee houses, and these too can be seen as forerunners of the modern restaurant.

2 Antonin Carême (1784–1833) is frequently cited as the original celebrated chef. As well as being famous for producing elaborate centre-pieces spun-out of sugar that decorated the dining table, he wrote on gastronomy, codified recipes and travelled widely to the great aristocratic kitchens of Europe.

3 Present day Tokyo, with its estimated 200,000 eating establishments may well be the twenty-first century equivalent of nineteenth century Paris.

4 The annual statistics produced by government agencies in France, Canada, Japan, Australia, Sweden, Germany, USA

and so on, each indicate rates of consumption in cafes, hotels, restaurants and the like. From the late 1960s onwards, these statistical portraits show rates of food and beverage consumption on an ever increasingly upward steep curve. The food industries have become one of the largest sectors in the national economies of industrialized societies (Nestle, 2002).

Bibliography

Bell, D. and Valentine, G. (1997). *Consuming Geographies*. London: Routledge.

Brillat-Savarin, J.A. (1825/1970). *The Physiology of Taste*. New York: Liveright.

Counihan, C. and Van Esterik, P. (Eds) (1997). *Food and Culture*. New York: Routledge.

Douglas, M. (1970). *Purity and Danger: An Analysis of Concepts of Pollution and Taboo*. London: Routledge and Kegan Paul.

Douglas, M. (1979). Les structures du culinaire. *Communications* **31**, 145–170.

Eagleton, T. (1998). In *The Eagleton Reader* (S. Regan, Ed.). Oxford: Blackwell.

Eco, U. (1973). Social life as sign. In *Structuralism* (D. Robey, Ed.). Oxford: Oxford University Press.

Elias, N. (1978). *The Civilizing Process*. Oxford: Blackwell Publishers.

Felski, R. (1995). *The Gender of Modernity*. Camb. Mass: Harvard University Press.

Finkelstein, J. (1989). *Dining Out: A Sociology of Modern Manners*. Oxford: Polity Press.

Freud, S. (1900). The Interpretation of Dreams. In *The Standard Edition of the Complete Psychological Works of Sigmund Freud* (James Strachey, trans and Ed.), 24 Vols. Hogarth Press, Vol. 4, 1952–1974, p. 147.

Furetière, A. (1708/1978). *Dictionnaire Universel*. Paris: Parmentier.

Griffiths, S. and Wallace, J. (Eds) (1998). *Consuming Passions: Food in the Age of Anxiety*. Manchester: Manchester University Press.

Levenstein, H. (1988). *Revolution at the Table: The Transformation of the American Diet*. New York: Oxford University Press.

Lingis, A. (1994). *Abuses*. Berkeley: University of California Press.

Mayle, P. (1991). *A Year in Provence*. New York: Random.

Nestle, M. (2002). *Food Politics: How the Food Industry Influences Nutrition and Health*. Berkeley: University of California Press.

Pillsbury, R. (1990). *From Boarding House to Bistro: The American Restaurant Then and Now*. Boston: Unwin Hyman.

Sennett, R. (1994). *Flesh and Stone: The Body and the City in Western Civilization*. London: Faber and Faber.

Simmel, G. (1950). *The Sociology of Georg Simmel*. Chicago: University of Chicago Press.

Spang, R. (2000). *The Invention of the Restaurant*. Camb. Mass: Harvard University Press.

Trillin, C. (2002). The red and the white. *The New Yorker Food Issue*. August 19–26.

The shock of the new: a sociology of *nouvelle cuisine*

Roy C. Wood

This chapter offers a sociological analysis of *nouvelle cuisine*. *Nouvelle cuisine* presents an interesting focus for the sociologist concerned with the relationship between food and culture. It has held culinary pre-eminence among certain sections of the middle class and is claimed by many commentators to have revo-lutionized the provision of French *haute cuisine* in the commercial hotel and catering industry.

Introduction

In recent years there has been a growth of academic sociological interest in the cultural significance of food and eating. Building on the early work of such pioneers of the field as Lévi-Strauss (1966) and Mary Douglas (1975), much of this research has been directed towards the everyday meanings attached to food in (mainly) domestic settings (Murcott, 1983). While of value to both the general theorist curious to elaborate the symbolic significance of food and eating and the home economist/social nutritionist concerned with issues of family constitution, research to date has rarely taken as its focus the wider question of dining outside the home and is further limited by a characteristic focus on small samples of working-class subjects and 'everyday' food.

There are, of course, exceptions to this general tendency, notably Mennell's (1985) seminal historical study of the comparative development of British and French cuisine, Driver's (1983) semi-academic account of British domestic and restaurant cuisine in the period from 1940 and Finkelstein's (1989) analysis of restaurant dining. However, on the whole dining outside the home has been ignored by sociologists of food and eating and the commercial provision of food has suffered particular neglect.

This chapter offers a sociological analysis of *nouvelle cuisine* in the UK context. For many, *nouvelle cuisine* is regarded as the most rarefied of all forms of *haute cuisine*, epitomizing gastronomic excellence and good taste. At the same time, *nouvelle cuisine* has been a frequent focus for satirists. It is 'A child's portion served to an adult' (Beard and McKie, 1987). Even Paul Bocuse, a chef associated with the nouvelle style, has allegedly stated that 'The so-called *nouvelle cuisine* usually means not enough on your plate and too much on your bill' (quoted in Green, 1985). *Nouvelle cuisine* thus attracts adulatory enthusiasm and satirical derision in seemingly equal proportions. However, that it should attract such attention at all is significant since the role of French *haute cuisine* in the culinary life of the UK remains restricted to a small social circle.

The contention of this chapter is that *nouvelle cuisine* is important as a social and culinary phenomenon, the importance for sociological analysis deriving from its adoption by certain sections of the middle class. Further, in all its many forms, *nouvelle cuisine* remains above all else experimental: it has seemingly neither become institutionalized as the successor to, or next stage of development, in conventional *haute cuisine*, nor been wholly rejected, though some writers detect that the very concept is on the wane. In this respect, the *nouvelle* style provides a useful focus for analysing processes of change in *haute cuisine*, particularly in the light of *nouvelle cuisine*'s position in both restaurant and domestic dining.

Finally, the *nouvelle* style is of interest because of the nature of the market relationship that exists between producer and consumer. *Nouvelle cuisine* is very much a producer's product, yet it has been embraced by an audience willing to be dictated to by suppliers – not perhaps altogether unusual in a world where the power of the latter is routinely used to mould consumer tastes, but curious in that the market for *nouvelle cuisine* is normally regarded as one characterized by considerable discrimination and exacting demands.

The characteristics of *nouvelle cuisine*

Use of the term *nouvelle cuisine* is, ironically, not new but can be traced to the 1730s and cookery books of the chefs Menon, Marin and La Chapelle (Mennell, 1985, p. 163). It resurfaced in the 1880s when it was associated with the generation of chefs dominated by Escoffier. In recent time, the term *nouvelle cuisine* has been associated with the championing by French food writers Henri Gault and Christian Millau of styles of cookery practised by, *inter alia*, Paul Bocuse, Michel Guerard and Roger Vergé. According to Barr and Levy (1984), Gault and Millau christened this style of cookery in a 1973 article entitled 'Vive la *nouvelle cuisine* française' published in their gastronomic magazine. Despite the diversity of culinary styles represented by the work of alleged practitioners of *nouvelle cuisine*, in a later (1976) publication, Gault and Millau identified 10 characteristics common to this gastronomic phenomenon (Mennell, 1985, pp. 163–164).

(a) Unnecessary complication in cookery was rejected and, in respect of technique, led to a favouring of poaching, baking and steaming.
(b) Cooking times for many commodities (notably fish, seafood, game birds, veal, green vegetables and paté) were reduced, aiming, so Mennell argues, to 'reveal forgotten flavours' (1985, p. 163) as a result of more naturalistic cooking.
(c) The best ingredients were used wherever possible, purchased at markets daily.
(d) Menus were shortened and the long menus of large hotels abandoned.

Hospitality, Leisure & Tourism Series

(e) Strong marinades for meat were rejected and game was served fresh not high, a trend doubted in its effect by Barr and Levy on the grounds of the reduced palatability likely to result from such a practice (1984, p. 63).

(f) Rich and heavy sauces were eliminated, especially béchamel and espagnole. Use of flour roux was regarded with disdain and sauces were made by reducing cooking liquids and finishing with cream or butter while making wider use of herbs, lemon juice and vinegar in the dressing of dishes in an effort both to bring out the flavours of the commodities uses and avoid a perceived tendency in existing French *haute cuisine* to mask poor ingredients with heavy sauces.

(g) Inspiration for new dishes was drawn from regional cookery rather than Parisian *haute cuisine*, though this tended to preclude heavy peasant-style dishes such as casseroles.

(h) Modern kitchen technology was used, if only experimentally. Food processors, microwave ovens and the use of frozen foods were not precluded.

(i) The dietetic implications of food were an important element of menu planning. Red meats (excepting lamb) were frowned upon and frying was used, if at all, only sparingly. Use of salt and sugar was reduced.

(j) The new chefs had creativity in abundance and a premium was placed on constant innovation and experimentation.

To this list Mennell (1985, p. 164) adds a further point – that most of the *nouveaux cuisiniers* identified by Gault and Millau were chef-patrons, owners of their own businesses. Mennell accounts for this in terms of a *general* gastronomic rebellion against the culinary orthodoxy of Escoffier, as enshrined in the international hotel industry (an orthodoxy that was and still is the primary influence on culinary education and practice, at least in the UK) and the more *specific* early association and training of several leading practitioners of *nouvelle cuisine*. Mennell writes:

> Several of its leaders were students of the great Fernand Point at the Pyramide in Vienne, and went on like him to own relatively small restaurants in provincial towns. Perhaps it was inevitable that the bureaucratic pressures and accounting preoccupations within modern hotel

chains would today make them unpromising sites for cooking at the highest level, however suitable an environment they had given Escoffier. Accountancy plays little part in *nouvelle cuisine*. By its nature it is expensive: it requires the finest ingredients and is extremely labour intensive. (Mennell, 1985, p. 164).

For writers such as Mennell (1985), Barr and Levy (1984) and Levy (1986), *nouvelle cuisine* is the latest stage in the procedural development of French *haute cuisine*. The concept of 'process' is preferred to labels implying more radical change since it is argued that, historically, there is a discernible tendency for the development of cuisines to be characterized by an overall trend towards increasing refinement – manifest in *nouvelle cuisine* through the aforementioned simplicity in the use of fewer ingredients with more discrimination, enhancement of natural flavours in cooking and the production of dishes which are more differentiated in flavour because they are less masked by the use of basic sauces (Mennell, 1985, p. 165).

Acceptance of this view of culinary development is not unproblematic for it encourages the idea of such development as inevitable. It is a status quo view and one that has led Murcott (1986) to detect foodie partisanship in Mennell's (1985) work (that is a lack of academic detachment for the subject matter). Such criticism is not without foundation. A fundamental problem with the position of Mennell and other commentators is their failure to disengage fully the social and nutritional/culinary dimensions to Gault and Millau's '10-point plan'. The 10 characteristics of *nouvelle cuisine* do not simply embody principles of *culinary* philosophy and technique but reflect a range of social values and concerns that go unelaborated. For convenience, these will be discussed in the remainder of this chapter in terms of the social construction, social production and social consumption of *nouvelle cuisine*, with the aim being to illuminate the cultural rather that the culinary basis of this style of cookery.

The social construction of *nouvelle cuisine*

In social as well as in culinary and nutritional terms, *nouvelle cuisine* has been presented as superior to both previous traditions in *haute cuisine* and other forms of food co-existing contemporarily with it. In a moral sense, *nouvelle cuisine* is not only intrinsically 'good', it is the very best there is. In much the same way as working-class mothers in a study by Murcott (1982) viewed 'cooked dinners' (comprising meat, potatoes, vegetables and gravy) as vital to the maintenance of family health, promoters of *nouvelle cuisine* emphasize the goodness of the food and its centrality to the well-being of those who possess a refined palate. Such goodness derives from the purity of the ingredients employed and the methods used in cooking them.

The 'goodness' of *nouvelle cuisine* in this context reflects well-documented social anthropological evidence highlighting the preoccupation in many social milieux with concepts of impurity. To this extent, *nouvelle cuisine* can be seen as akin to a social purity movement, concerned with recapturing some golden age cookery and/or achieving some rapport with that which is held to be truly representative of nature and naturalness – both elements being signalled in the emphasis on simplicity and freshness and also in the utilization by chefs of regional (country) cuisine for inspiration. This 'back to Eden' analogy must not be overdrawn, yet appeals to a more natural past in cookery are an important element in the promotion of *nouvelle cuisine*.

This can be seen by taking a second example of the way in which *nouvelle cuisine* is accorded superiority by it proponents: by the emphasis place on the exceptional creativity and artistry of chefs and their products. Constant innovation, experimentation and self-sacrifice by chef practitioners are all factors advanced in support of the proposition that *nouvelle cuisine* is not merely cookery but involved 'art' beyond ordinary culinary craft. Not only the production but the presentation of *nouvelle cuisine* is depicted as an artistic activity lying somewhere between painting and sculpture. The use of the finest ingredients and the best skills necessitates use of the best display techniques. Thus as Levy (1986) notes, sauces are placed under, never over, the food. To this might be added the observation that *nouvelle cuisine* dishes tend to be highly sculpted, a bas-relief in a sea of colour (though the ubiquitous and clichéd octagonal plates that characterized early '*nouvelle* photography' seem to have fallen into relative disuse).

In the mythology of *nouvelle cuisine*, chefs' artistry is elevated to a new status as Levy shows:

> ... the arrangement of the plate became the duty (and pleasure) of the cook, not the waiter – and food as art was born. Silver service died, as chefs everywhere made pictures on plates. (Levy, 1986, p. 139)

Mennell (1985, pp. 144–145) argues a view similar to the above while at the same time cautioning against 'great men' theories of cuisine and supplying detailed evidence of artistic preoccupations in *haute cuisine* going back several hundred years. Therefore, the putative artistic superiority and innovation of the *nouvelle* style relative to previous traditions in *haute cuisine* is, in historical terms, nothing more than the most recent manifestation of established practice.

Earlier in this section, an analogy was drawn between *nouvelle cuisine* and social purity movements. One characteristic of the latter is that members are bound together to some extent by perceived threats of disapprobation and disapproval from wider society, however real such threats may or may not be. To some extent, this attitude is found in many writings on *nouvelle cuisine*. Here a distinction is made between 'true' *nouvelle cuisine* and 'genuine' practitioners and sham *nouvelle cuisine* and charlatans, as in the following remark by Levy (1986, p. 139).

> The pioneers of *nouvelle cuisine* stressed the freshness of the ingredients. Second rate imitators stressed their expense. *Nouvelle cuisine* was concerned with health – avoiding refined flour, reducing fats and shunning fried food. The band-wagon jumpers-on lowered calories by making portions minute. *Nouvelle cuisine* chefs like to experiment with new ingredients and techniques. Their sedulous apers valued novelty above all else.

A similar view is taken by Mennell (1985, p. 164).

> Perhaps it is unavoidable that as its ideas are adopted by lesser talents in less liberal contexts, *nouvelle cuisine* too will undergo routinization and become a dogma.

Hospitality, Leisure & Tourism Series

Such responses emphasize the extent to which the moral integrity and superiority of *nouvelle cuisine* is seen as liable to dilution through the cheapening of content and method and the degradation of form. Attempts to maintain the integrity of what amounts to an ideal of *nouvelle cuisine* reinforces its exclusivity. In the strictest sense, however, *nouvelle cuisine* cannot be seen as completely analogous to the 'ideal type' social purity movement because, as the preceding quotations suggest, perceived threats of dilution come less from outside the community of professional chefs than from within it.

Here one of the many paradoxes of *nouvelle cuisine* is encountered, namely that the emphasis on creativity and individuality, while embracing *generally* systematic principles, has so far eschewed the *specific* systemization of dishes and recipes. No formalized repertoire of dishes that represents *nouvelle cuisine* exists. Many practitioners have, of course, published their recipes but to date there is an absence of anything approaching the status of those manuals that enshrine the orthodoxy of Escoffierian cookery for apprentice and practising chefs, for example the *Larousse Gastronomique*.

While too much should not be made of the point, it does seem likely that any such systemization is unlikely to occur. If precise culinary and recipe standards were set then this would create an operational as opposed to theoretical orthodoxy and *nouvelle cuisine* would lose what makes it distinctive, since constant innovation, creativity and experimentation would have been abandoned in favour of a flexible nucleus of 'standard' dishes.

Perceived threats of dilution from within the professional community of *nouveaux cuisiniers* is perhaps best understood as a manifestation of competition between practitioners, serving as a constant reminder of the need to be 'true' to the general characteristics of the art. At the same time, insistence of adherence to general principles serves not only as a mode of critical censure but as a way of further differentiating *nouvelle* practitioners from other chefs and cooks, the 'sedulous apers' of lesser skill and talent. In both cases, the threat of dilution forms part of the rhetoric of individualism that surrounds the production of *nouvelle cuisine*. It is to this that attention now turns.

The social production of *nouvelle cuisine*

As shown in the previous section, *nouvelle cuisine* is not produced in a social vacuum. Culinary production is conceptualized and executed in a social context which in turn reflects the values, beliefs and ideologies of the producers. This is what is meant here by the social production of *nouvelle cuisine*. At the heart of this process is the concept of individualism. Individualism plays a crucial role in the rhetoric and self-image of *nouveaux cuisiniers*. This is also true of those consumers of *nouvelle cuisine*, as will be shown later.

The rhetoric of individualism that surrounds the production of *nouvelle cuisine* is embodied in a set of tightly interlocking mythologies (in the Barthesian sense) (Barthes, 1972) about the organization of culinary production. The first of these concerns the standard account of the origins of modern *nouvelle cuisine* which supposedly lie in the efforts of an initially small group of independent chef-patrons who, dissatisfied and/or despondent with the potential for practising their craft in the highly standardized settings of large hotels, chose alternative routes to self-fulfilment, being joined, as the fashionability of *nouvelle cuisine* spread, by similar entrepreneurs.

The concept of 'entrepreneur' plays a significant if submerged role in the mythology of *nouvelle cuisine*, for the practitioner is hardly ever an entrepreneur through choice. Rather, the business-owning route is forced upon the practitioner: *nouveaux cuisiniers* are portrayed as unappreciated artists, frustrated with an establishment that does not understand them and forced (initially at least) into realizing their talents in the restaurant-industry equivalent of a garret. This is the chef as individualistic hero and entrepreneur, risking all for his or her talent. It is also a highly questionable view even when extended, in modified form, to embrace those chefs employed by others (sympathetic to new cookery) in small restaurants and hotels.

While it may be true that the varieties of new cookery are more readily found in small owner-managed operations (irrespective of whether the chef is owner or employee), there is no evidence to suggest that such businesses are any more or less risky than any owner-managed operation in the UK catering trade. The implicit view that *nouveaux cuisiniers* risk all for their art in becoming chef-patrons, and that this is a key factor differentiating them from other (less talented) chefs, does not bear scrutiny. Indeed, as Chivers (1973) has pointed out, the desire to own a business is widespread not only among chefs but certain other catering occupations as well. Nevertheless, the concept of individualism applies no less in the analysis of *nouveaux cuisiniers* than other chefs. It is essentially a *petit-bourgeois* notion of individualism embodying the notion of the 'little' man or woman attempting to conserve space for themselves in a world in which both state and society are increasingly seen as impinging upon their liberties.

In the context of the social production of *nouvelle cuisine*, this can, secondly, be further illustrated by reference to the self-perception of *nouveaux cuisiniers* in respect of the rest of the culinary profession and catering trade. As previously observed, *nouvelle cuisine* chefs are seen as being possessed of exceptional creativity, a creativity that marks them out from the majority of their peers. No systematic explanation of these exceptional talents has yet been advanced. What is made clear is that such creativity cannot flourish in a culinary establishment so clearly linked, historically with upper and upper-middle class values that assumed pre-eminence at the end of the nineteenth century and has led to the perpetuation of a culinary aristocracy that derives its authority from the power and control it has consistently exerted over professional training and occupational culture. Each initiate's career must progress through a relatively clearly defined number of stages in an occupational hierarchy predicated more on position, status and time-serving than on creative talent and innovation.

If the culinary system established by Escoffier reflects the values of the old European aristocracies and *haute bourgeoisie*, then *nouvelle cuisine* is the cuisine of the new and essentially provincial middle class. The tendency of *nouveaux cuisiniers* to turn from metropolitan to regional sources for culinary inspiration is a reflection of conscious preoccupations not only with 'naturalness' but with markets. It is no coincidence that the French progenitors of modern *nouvelle cuisine* were themselves of largely *petit-bourgeois* origin and set up business in the provinces. The characteristics of *nouvelle cuisine* so carefully identified by Gault and Millau reflect the sensibilities of men whose livelihoods were ultimately bound up with class and geographical considerations. In the UK context, as elsewhere, time has perhaps eroded the significance of such associations, though it is worth noting that many of those practitioners of *nouvelle cuisine* who are judged among 'the best' are based as much in the provinces as in metropolitan areas.

The combination of ideas of risk and entrepreneurship constitutes a potent force in the self-perception of *nouveaux cuisiniers* and, in turn, their perceptions of others. This, not only is the chef-patron a heroically creative artistic refugee, but one who is prepared to abandon the 'subsidy' to his talent supplied by the culinary establishment (and its conventions) and élite patronage, linking personal reputation to entrepreneurial flair.

Risk and entrepreneurship combined with artistic freedom are all expressions of the rhetoric of individualism that surrounds the production of *nouvelle cuisine*. All three are closely linked to a fourth concept, that of 'responsibility'. The producer of *nouvelle cuisine* as chef-businessman takes full responsibility for production, for the quality of the product and for the standards of delivery of the product to the consumer, all central tenets of modern *petit-bourgeois* culture with its emphasis on personal service and customized products. Waiting staff are, allegedly, marginalized.

In conventional restaurants, the purchase of a meal also entails the purchase of service, traditionally supplied by an intermediary – the waiter/waitress. In *nouvelle cuisine*, the role of waiting staff is reduced, with the chef taking skills from them, denying them one of their principle functions – the arrangement of food on the plate of the consumer. Consumers do not participate in the rituals of dining out in a restaurant serving *nouvelle cuisine* for the service, as conventionally construed. What might be termed 'the food is less than brilliant but the service is outstanding' syndrome disappears under *nouvelle cuisine* which, with the close control of the chef, approximates to a solo form of performing art: the chef reappropriates his or her skills at the expense of the waiter who is deskilled.

As part of the mythology of *nouvelle cuisine*, it works rather well to suggest that chefs have reasserted themselves, put waiters in their place and drawn closer to the consumer is assuming responsibility for their work. In fact, if anything, the marginalization of the waiter under *nouvelle cuisine* can be seen as part of a much wider trend in the catering trade towards concentration of capital in the kitchen. In the case of *nouvelle cuisine*, this may be human capital as opposed to plant and equipment, but the process is not in any way extraordinary. Waiters have been undergoing a process of marginalization for years, the trend towards plated service going back at least three decades. Further, the demand for silver service skills persists at virtually all levels of the catering industry and, in many types of operation, waiters have acquired new work tasks including, in many instances, those involving cookery.

In this section, the ideological context in which *nouvelle cuisine* is produced has been explored in terms of the mythological qualities – values, beliefs, images – imputed to the producers, both by themselves and others. What needs to be stressed here is that the extent to which the topics discussed are 'true' or 'false' is largely irrelevant and probably impossible to establish, although the extent to which some are potentially more or less accurate can be determined. What is significant is the extent to which as a body of folklore, the themes examined support an image of *nouvelle cuisine* and its practitioners which links closely to consumers' concerns, as the following section shows.

The social consumption of *nouvelle cuisine*

Both in its production and consumption *nouvelle cuisine* is a middle-class cuisine. As Barr and Levy (1984, p. 65) note, eating *nouvelle cuisine* displays one's income. There is nothing unusual about this: participating in the ritual of public dining at the higher levels has always been a way of evidencing distinctiveness (Riley, 1984). However, within the bourgeoisie, such methods of marking distinctiveness have seemingly been more closely directed to a display of refinement and good taste primarily for the benefit of those similarly placed in the class structure (Riley, 1984, p. 103). Financial security, that is the ability to afford *haute cuisine*, is taken for granted and financial status is marginalized in favour of expressions of class solidarity predicated on shared assumptions about 'good food' and 'good taste'.

Nouvelle cuisine is slightly different. Its consumption is no less an implicit expression of financial security, for *nouvelle cuisine* is very expensive, but the 'value ratio' between money and the content and quality of *nouvelle cuisine* expresses brasher values. They are values which somewhat paradoxically express individuals' membership of the middle classes while at the same time distancing themselves from it, for *nouvelle cuisine* is the cuisine of the *arriviste* middle classes, predominantly the young and upwardly mobile with high disposable incomes and a desire to differentiate themselves from both the established (usually older) and competing class factions.

Eating *nouvelle cuisine* food does not so much display a person's level of income but more the manner in which it was acquired. Favouring *nouvelle cuisine* entails elements of risk on the part of the consumer as it does on the part of the producer: the risk of lampooning that comes less from the general public than a variety of commentators who, frequently, both promote and sneer at the new cooking: and the risk that bedevils all catering, namely that there will be shortfall between expectations and reality. These minor risk elements are an important way of cementing an affinity between chefs and their public. The basis of this is a mutual empathy deriving from a shared mythology that each is different, slightly superior, part of the (coming) mainstream of their professional and/or class group and yet still slightly peripheral, independent, creative and experimental.

The naturalness of *nouvelle cuisine* also performs an extremely important function in terms of class and economic values. The stress is on *nouvelle cuisine* as restrained, aesthetic gourmet cooking and traditional *haute cuisine* as excessive, ersatz and gourmandesque. *Nouvelle cuisine* may be expensive but symbolically it is not the food of the gastronomically greedy. The naturalness/health motifs de-emphasize guilt aspects imputed to traditional *haute cuisine* with its emphasis on richness, adulteration and luxuriance embedded in a complex system of excessive ritual.

Nouvelle cuisine is a sanitized gastronomy, the artistry of which is naturalistic and representational, redolent of the Pre-Raphaelite Brotherhood's attempt in the nineteenth century to return to more basic, pastoral values and truth in colour and form. For consumers, it is the non-vegetarian version of 'eating virtue' (Atkinson, 1983). It is also the cuisine of the 'can do' generation, of the bullish middle-class professionals. And here perhaps lies the greatest of the paradoxes that is *nouvelle cuisine*, for while it is essentially valorized as a chef's medium, the new cookery is intrinsically ephemeral and insubstantial. Anybody *can* do it, as is testified by the extent and frequency to which *nouvelle cuisine* is transported into the home:

> … think what it means for the home cook when something only needs 40 seconds cooking. It means your friend can be with you from preparation to table. It turns cooking into theatre. (Barr and Levy, 1984, p. 65).

The mythologies that surround the social production of *nouvelle cuisine* are far from invalidated because of its transferability between restaurant and home. On the contrary, its essentially democratic accessibility confers all the qualities associated with the professional producers of *nouvelle cuisine* on the consumer-amateur. That anybody can cook naturally, artistically and creatively if they follow general principles that do not detract from the qualities of the professional purveyor but buttresses them, for imitation is the sincerest form of flattery and the possibility of imitation arises from the leadership of the professionals. *Nouvelle cuisine* restores cults of the personality as a central feature of gastronomy after a period in which, post-Escoffier, culinary Taylorism had disassociated the means of production from the producers.

Conclusions

A charitable interpretation of prior academic and quasi-academic interest in French *haute cuisine* in general and *nouvelle cuisine* in particular would be that it is motivated by a concern for a widespread democratic uplifting of people's taste (Murcott, 1988). Less charitably, the expenditure of so much energy on analysing the supposed quality of *haute cuisine* can be seen not only as élitist (in ignoring popular cuisine) but as neglectful of more important questions concerning the production of *haute cuisine*, such as exploitation of the labour used in producing it and the extent to which the persistence of a dominant culinary paradigm encourages chauvinism and ethnocentricity. More important yet is the 'true' nature of *nouvelle cuisine*. Its promoters are guilty of extraordinary intellectual liberties. Ignoring the dietary patterns of the majority, Barr and Levy write:

> It looked like a fashion, but something *had* happened. Cooking had moved into its next phase. The cooking of the industrial revolution was over. The North had lost. The sunnier Catholic and Eastern countries won the battle of the estomac. (1984, p. 64).

Similarly both writers argue that:

> Some fuddy-duddies still think that *nouvelle cuisine* is a fad that will be replaced. (Barr and Levy, 1984, p. 65).

However, in another article, Levy (1986, p. 143) detects that *nouvelle cuisine* contains within it its own seeds of destruction. It is difficult to take seriously these outpourings on *nouvelle cuisine*, if only because in analytic terms they are part of the problem rather than the solution. *Nouvelle cuisine*, to more so than its *haute cuisine* predecessors, is a social construct rather than a culinary one, reflecting the narrow concerns of, and changes within, the middle class. *Nouvelle cuisine* is the fish and chips, hamburger, pizza and pancake of the middle classes. It may become an integral part of the culinary scene but it will always be on the periphery of 'serious' food and eating, remaining far more interesting for its sociological, rather than gastronomic significance.

Bibliography

Atkinson, P. (1983). Eating Virtue. In *The Sociology of Food and Eating* (A. Murcott, Ed.). Gower.

Barr, A. and Levy, P. (1984). *The Official Foodie Handbook*. London: Ebury Press.

Barthes, R. (1973). *Mythologies*. London: Paladin.

Beard, H. and McKie, R. (1987). *Cooking*. London: Methuen.

Chivers, T. (1973). The proletarianization of a service worker. *Sociological Review* **21**, 633–656.

Douglas, M. (Ed.) (1975). Deciphering a meal. In *Implicit Meanings*. London: Routledge and Kegan Paul.

Driver, C. (1983). *The British at Table 1940–1980*. London: Chatto and Windus.

Finkelstein, J. (1989). *Dining Out: A Sociology of Modern Manners*. Cambridge: Polity Press.

Green, J. (1985). *Consuming Passions*. London: Sphere.

Lévi-Strauss, C. (1966). The culinary triangle. *New Society* **22**, 166.

Levy, P. (1986). *Out to Lunch*. London: Chatto and Windus.

Mennell, S. (1985). *All Manners of Food: Eating and Taste in England and France from the Middle Ages to the Present*. Oxford: Blackwell.

Murcott, A. (1982). On the social significance of the 'cooked dinner' in South Wales. *Social Science Information* **21**, 677–696.

Murcott, A. (Ed.) (1983). *The Sociology of Food and Eating*. Farnborough: Gower.

Murcott, A. (1986). Review of S. Mennell. All manners of food: eating and taste in England and France from the middle ages to the present. *Sociology* **20**, 645–646.

Murcott, A. (1988). Sociological and social anthropological approaches to food and eating. *World Review of Nutrition and Dietetics* **66**, 1–40.

Riley, M. (1984). Hotels and group identity. *Tourism Management* **5** (2), 102–109.

Reproduced from Wood R.C. (1991) The schock of the new. *International Journal of Consumer Studies and Home Economics* **15**, 327–328. Reprinted by permission of the Publishers, Blackwell Scientific Ltd.

CHAPTER 6

Contemporary lifestyles: the case of wine

Marion Demossier

In the study of alimentary changes and of their relationship to taste, wine can be analysed sociologically
as one of the most complex and heterogeneous types
of food. Yet despite the vast outpouring of literature
devoted to the analysis of food consumption, it is a
subject that has largely been ignored, even though
wine stands out as a distinct object of sociological
inquiry because of its syncretic nature. Wine has
long been reputed for its nutritional values and has
frequently been defined as a potent, spiritual substance and a masculine beverage. As bread and wine
are among the principal elements of Christian the-
ology, the consumption of wine relates to the tensions
between excesses in alcohol consumption and the
Judeo Christian religious belief of self-control. Historically, the cultivation of wine was inextricably
linked to the religious uses of wine and it cannot just
be understood as an ordinary commodity. Yet if its
production was intrinsically linked to religious communities, its consumption was from the earliest times

an object of intense social exchanges and conveyed a real sense of prestige. Wine can be described as a food for hierarchy, and it contributes to the hierarchization of society.

This phenomenon is revealed within the increasingly wide range of wines available to the consumer which responds, in part, to the growing diversification of drinkers and their desires, contributing in turn to changes in tastes. Unlike almost any other type of alimentary product, wine requires the use of the five senses to fully appreciate its qualities. It is one of the rare products in which the correct way to taste it has been codified through guides or literary works. This was illustrated perfectly by the French oenologist, Jean Lenoir, who created in 1985 a box 'Le Nez du Vin' with 54 different aromas that are supposedly essential to successful wine-tasting, demonstrating the extreme sophistication of tastes in wine consumption.

If we want to understand the nature and the influences on contemporary culinary taste expressed in commercial restaurant settings, it is necessary to acknowledge the economic, cultural and social dimensions of wine drinking. Major changes in these factors have shaped the way we think about consuming wine. As a result, it is essential to examine to what extent taste is influenced by social conditions or whether personal taste is less constrained and can be considered an expression of individualism. Three major areas of discussion are identified to help us to understand the nature of the changes between taste and wine consumption in a public and commercial space such as the restaurant, in contrast to the private setting of domestic consumption:

- The tensions between homogeneization and diversification of tastes in wine consumption at an international level.
- Eating and drinking out as a social, occasional and festive space where tastes and all manners of food are inextricably linked.
- The construction of the wine drinker and his/her desires as an object of social enquiry.

Changes in wine consumption and culture have had a major impact on definitions of taste. At an international level, it has followed some of the major processes affecting the food sector more generally. Tensions between globalization and localism combined with homogenization and differentiation define the contrasting trends at the core of wine consumption and tastes. Firstly, the international wine industry has experienced a concentration at an economic level with ever larger companies whose size, branding, distribution channels and general marketing play an ever more important role in determining success. International companies such as Gallo or Orlando Wyndham are major players in the global wine sector. The Australian wine industry, for example, is dominated by just three large companies (BRL Hardy, Southcorp and Forster's). The growth of multinational and transnational corporate enterprises is a powerful force for global convergence of values and behaviour, especially in relation to taste. Secondly, these economic transformations have permitted a substantial increase in the quantity and the quality of wines produced, and one of the effects of growing competition has been the transformation of wine into a high quality product that is increasingly sold through chains or supermarkets. It is equally true to say that restaurants now have closer contacts with the wine industry through wholesalers and intermediaries or even directly to the producers. The idea of access to a wider choice is an integral part of the tasting experience. As the multiple retailer must cater for the widest taste and achieve a high inventory turnover, the restaurant has to acknowledge the different needs of the modern consumer.

The process of globalization has, however, privileged the market for premium wines which dominate the international wine sector, while it has become difficult for small producers to have access to the wider economic market. Wine is now associated with brands, marketing and standardization, which are among the principal advantages offered by well-managed companies. In this globalization of the wine economy, the New World has a lot to offer. Its formula – sun plus technology equals great wine – has captured the hearts and minds of a public that finds it hard to come to grips with the concept of *terroir*, by which the French and other world producers signal their excellence. A war seems to confront *terroir* against grapes or variety of vines. *Terroir*, which is almost untranslatable in another language, could be defined today as an ongoing construction of a collective representation of the past through the work of the producers and it refers, for the consumer, to an area of terrain, usually quite small, whose soil and microclimate impart distinctive qualities to food products. *Terroir* could be identified as an area that produces a *grand cru* (high premium) or a particularly distinctive wine in which European producers dominate the market. It could also be said that a certain wine has a *goût*, or taste of its particular *terroir*. Specific gustative characteristics will be associated to its taste. A *Volnay Premier cru* for instance will be described as fruity, astringent, rich and flowered.

In the global marketing war, *terroir* represents certain standards of quality often linked with artisanal principles of craftsmanship (Bell and Valentine, 1997). Moreover, *terroir* relates back to greater diversity in tastes by putting emphasis on the combination between places, producers and diversity, while New World wines concentrate on the standardization of tastes in relation to specific grapes and on modern production techniques that permit the production of a consistent quality of wine over the years. According to French scholars Chiva (1985) and Puisais (1987), one of the consequences is an impoverishment of taste which means that only three basic tastes are today recognized (saltiness, sweetness and sharpness).

Without going so far, the question of the changing nature of tastes in wines is also largely dependent on the debates about diversification and differentiation in the context of the so-called globalization of tastes. First and foremost, wine production has greatly diversified not only following the recognition at a European level of a greater number of *appellations* (denomination of origin) which functions as a kind of trademarks, but also through the creation of new types of wine such as Wicked Wines which aim at young people or organic wines responding to specific segments of the market. It is undeniable that wine is a product category where variety is valued. Accompanying this increasingly diversified wine market, there has been a clear need for more information relevant to the consumers. Wine culture since the 1980s has boomed and has transformed wine into a popular cultural object not confined solely to the consumption of the wealthy. Most commentators agree on the increasing power of education in wine consumption and the necessity to educate the wine drinker from an early age. From wine guides to items devoted to wine consumption, the wine industry has proliferated and penetrated into other sectors. It has also emerged as a place of passions and expression of identity. A telling example is offered by the library *Atheneum* devoted to wine literature and artefacts and located in Beaune (Burgundy) which claims to have passionate wine customers from all over the world, especially from America.

This wine culture is defined as part of a growing codification of 'all manners of food' (drink) and all manners of taste. Various schools of tastes have established themselves through the publication of specific guides such as the Guide Hachette in France or that of the American wine guru Robert Parker, and it is interesting to see that they reproduce to some extent, the divide between the rivals in the wine war. According to the editor of the Guide Hachette which sold 150,000 copies in France in 1990, the guides aim at different publics. Parker's book (circulation 60,000 in 1990 in France) is allegedly the work of a man with a school of thought and a very personal approach to wine; it is what we call an art book whereas the Guide Hachette does not have an *'esprit d'école'*. According to this analysis, French taste seems to obey to a more rigid framework as it seems that battles of tastes are also part of the process of legitimizing a codified rule of tasting. In the same vein, taste has become the object of intense debates which attest to the increasingly evanescent nature of the drinker who needs some landmarks. It is also recognized that notion of what constitutes a decent wine is judged very differently by each consumer or group of consumers.

The relationship between consumption and taste is central to any explanation of the changes affecting wine drinking culture. Greater affluence, increased leisure time and travel, and the development of common trade areas have changed and modified traditional drinking patterns. According to Smith and Soolgaard (1997), the modernization of societies has created a convergence in wine consumption. As traditional boundaries become blurred, the traditional north/south divide in the European alcoholic beverage market has declined and consumer preference for wine appears to be driven less by long-standing local and regional traditions, and more by growing acceptance of a wider choice. This analysis has been challenged by a number of scholars who have argued that modernization has taken different paths in different countries and that cultural factors should be taken into account when attempting any identification of wine consumption patterns. A recent report (2001) by Thor Norström concludes that today, despite modernization, there is still a wide variation between countries in most aspects of drinking patterns even if the Nordic countries are today 'former spirits countries' as beer and wine have become increasingly popular. In these changes, however, it is evident that modernization, homogenization and increasing self-awareness and self-control in health behaviour have played their role in the decline of alcohol consumption in Southern European countries.

However to argue that there is a clear convergence in patterns of consumption is going too far. Historical, economic, political, cultural and social factors all play an important role in relation to each national wine drinking culture and for every example of convergence, there are other signs of continuing distinctiveness. Attempts to identify new patterns of consumption or the 'new wine drinker', when differentiation within society has increased and when post-modern sociology keeps reminding us of the elusive nature of the consumer, are likely to be in vain. It is clear that the economic conditions of the 1980s and 1990s, the changes in taxation on alcohol, the ageing population, long-term government control over alcohol consumption, changes in women's lifestyle and growing public concerns over health have all challenged the position of wine as a national beverage in some of the traditional European countries. Yet a new wine drinker has emerged in different parts of the world and it seems that a moderate wine drinking culture and quest for variety is what defines him/her. The results of market research suggest that the new drinker can be identified as part of specific tribe with niche markets of certain customer type characterizing it. However, the new drinker's profile is still perceived as stable and specific in the context of an increasingly fragmented society and the democratization of wine drinking could be seen as the broad denominator in all these changes. Thus both differentiation and homogenization can, in part, explain changes in wine tastes.

A crucial element associated with wine drinking is the context in which it takes place. The key question is the extent to which the changes described above have affected the nature of the relationship between taste and wine consumption in a public and commercial space such as the restaurant, where taste is culturally shaped and socially controlled. First and foremost, eating out remains a public, out of the ordinary, visible and controlled social activity which can be more or less formalized, but is very often coupled with pleasure and sociability. Unlike beer and spirits, wine is usually consumed at the table, and wine consumption is associated with a variety of contexts, where sociability, celebration and taste stand out as extremely important motivational variables that are common to all cultural groups. It seems therefore that there is a certain consensus in relation to wine consumption when dining out. Wine can enhance the enjoyment of the meal and increase the overall satisfaction of the experience. It is thus part of this specific cultural experience. Indeed even if eating out symbolizes a socially significant temporally specific occasion, according to Warde and Martens (2000), the informal character of this ritualized activity has generally developed which means that different meanings have been given to wine consumption in relation to the various contexts. For example, drinking a glass of Barolo to accompany a pizza in the local restaurant does not have the same social connotation as tasting the same wine in the formal atmosphere of a fashionable Italian trattoria in New York.

If eating out has been democratized, it has nevertheless become an object of a wider differentiation in terms of the activities attached to it. From a night out with a cheap meal to a gourmet event, the variety of restaurants has increased with new strategies attached to the sector. This differentiation has to be emphasized through a pronounced symbolic and economic formalization, a greater variety, a higher quality combined with a more original and varied wine list. Food and restaurants have diversified to meet the challenge of the range of consumer demands (Cousin et al., 2001). In their typology of restaurants and cuisine, Cousin, Foskett and Gillespie identified 13 different types of eating out experience, which it could be argued, are matched by the same number of wine-tasting experiences. It is clear that there are a number of implications for how the restaurant is perceived and the extent to which its symbolic capacities are recognized by different social groups. Depending upon the nature and the emphasis put on the eating out experience, different strategies will accompany the choice of the setting, of the food and drinks to be ordered. It could be argued that the formalization of the whole experience of food and wine consumption will be in proportion to the quality, the prestige and the reputation of the restaurant. The tasting experience will, by the same token, have been enhanced. It is essential to take this differentiation into account as the tasting experience will take place in a more formalized environment and will require a sound knowledge of wine drinking culture. The contrast between everyday and festive food will also be strongly reinforced and the consumer will confirm this difference through consumption in his/her choice of wine.

As food and wine should complement each other, the wine list plays a major role in exploring the variety of tastes and in enhancing the quality of the tasting experience. Wine is more often considered as a food product than other beverages containing alcohol, and it is more readily paired with various food items. Matching food and wine remains above all the privilege of the gourmet and the gastronome. Mitchell and Greatorex (1989) noted that wine consumption in the UK occurs in the top socio-economic groups. Per capita consumption is, however, rapidly increasing in the middle group and the democratization of wine drinking is an increasingly established pattern. Good wines are still seen as a status symbol and tasting wines are part of this process of distinction. Experienced wine drinkers with a high cultural capital will have a sophisticated knowledge of the tastes associated with wine consumption and will be aware of the rules dictating the *bon goût*. Exploring the variety of tastes in wines will be part of the same experience as tasting food. Several different wines may accompany a meal, and a reputation for having an outstanding wine list can be a significant attraction on its own (Dodd, 1997). Some of today's best chefs have taken great care in the selection of their wine list as they want to make sure that their choice of wines will complement their cooking. To help them to achieve this, they are able to call upon the services of wine waiter, whose growing professional status and qualifications have made him/her the main actor in the combination of tastes advising chefs and consumers in their choice. Responding to increasing sophisticated tastes is a challenge for the wine waiter. The broadening of supply with the increasing availability of wines has all impacted on the modern wine list with the diversification in the range of consumer demands. The content and presentation of the wine list says a lot about a restaurant, and if buying wine in a restaurant setting is very often an impulse purchase, the wine list plays a major role in convincing consumers that they have made the right choice. Promotional and sales techniques are necessary to reinforce the customer's choice as wine is very often the product with the highest profit margin for the restaurant and it is important to have the cultural knowledge necessary to advise the customer.

In the setting of the restaurant, the *homo culinarius* has to obey to a codified set of rules concerning the combination of tastes in food and wine. Again, depending upon the type of setting, rules will be more or less reinforced or imposed upon the individual. A hierarchy of restaurants refers in general to a hierarchy of wines and thus a hierarchy of tastes. Our societies have more or less commonly agreed on the principles regulating the association of tastes in wine and dishes. However, the increasingly informal nature of the experience of eating out has challenged some of these pre-conceived ideas about the correct combination of food and wine. In general, food is selected first and then wines will be ordered to complement the meal. The main objective is to ensure harmony between the food and the beverage (Gillespie, 2001). Temperature, the palate, matching weights, intensity of both food and wine, flavour dominance, texture, cooking method, garnishes, sauces and accompaniments are all cited as characteristics to consider when creating such associations. However, it is very often the case that personal taste, price and experience are the key factors in the final choice. In this context, and despite the wide and detailed literature on each wine produced year after year, scholars agree in defining wine tasting as a subjective and individual experience where senses prevail. The palate being the mediator in grasping the four elements detected when drinking wine. Sweetness, saltiness, acidity and bitterness are all parts of this sensorial experience. If they are all used in various evaluations of wines, it could be said that they are not all of equal weight. Saltiness remains quite uncommon in wine and modern consumers have demonstrated a growing aversion towards strong tastes in wine, which refer to game, flesh or untamed natural or earthy flavours.

This could be interpreted in terms of what Norbert Elias (1978) has described as the 'civilizing process': our societies have entailed a strong and conscious effort to remove the distasteful from the sight of society. Even if it has developed differently from one country to another, this has been accompanied by an attraction for the softness of flavours and aromas, the discretion of smells and tastes. It could be said that the same process has affected wine consumption. The success of New World wines confirms that consumers have a preference for wines with 'fruity, light, easy to taste, quick to appreciate' characteristics while more traditional European wines are sometimes perceived as more complex to grasp. This division of tastes opposes the industrial and standardized wine which is characterized by its reliability and consistency in taste – referring to the grape and the vintage – to the more crafted traditional wine in which diversity and the unexpected prevail – place, age and nature of the grapes, name of the producer and vintage make it a less reliable product. Today, French wines, for example, have been challenged by American and Australian wines on the UK market attesting to the growing homogenization of tastes. Following the 'civilizing process', it could be argued that wines traditionally described as too 'animal' in their taste have been out of favour. The wine producing sector has witnessed the growing importance of fruity, light, new oaked wines for specific segments of the market. However, a minority of experienced drinkers still appreciate this type of wines and the recent auctions organized by Sotheby's demonstrate that there are still connoisseurs who are ready to spend substantial amount of money to obtain them. As the restaurant has been democratized, tastes in wine have become more homogenized, but they remain a space for the expression of differences.

When eating out, wine drinking appears to be the object of all manners of tastes for specific groups of individuals, while for others, it could be transformed into an intimidated and socially challenging experience. It seems that those with high cultural resources construct what they perceive to be a unique, original style through consumption of objects. They are more energetic in their attempts to individualize their consumption through authenticity and connoisseurship. By contrast, those with low cultural resources do not fear mass consumption because they embrace collective interpretations of taste. The category of innovators which has been identified in several publications on wine marketing corresponds to some extent to Holt's description. Innovators in the wine product category tend to drink wine more frequently, spend more money on wine and use different sources to obtain information about it. Their tastes are also more varied and complex. Two types of consumer can be defined: those highly involved in the choice and consumption of wine and those with lower involvement. As wine is complex compared to many other products, consumers with existing knowledge about wines in general are more likely to adopt a new wine and to follow advice.

For restaurateurs, wine innovators, who are defined as young and knowledgeable consumers, represent a possible market segment. Innovators are willing to spend more in a restaurant for wine than the non-innovators and they can be targeted to help increase a restaurant's profit from wine sales. However, they also need to be given more information as regards to which wines to taste. Despite the homogenization of tastes in wine drinking, specific types of wine are related to specific group profiles. In a recent article published in Harpers (2001), Jo Burzynska reported that six groups of consumers were identified: the classic connoisseur, generally being older with good knowledge of wine and a serious interest in the more traditional Old World wines; the enthusiast who buys into the traditional image of wine, is socially aspiring but lacking in confidence and knowledge and wants to buy the right wine, relating price to quality; the easily pleased who falls into the mass-market category and is often an older female wine drinker with no pretensions or ambitions and who sticks to familiar and often cheaper wines; the entertainers broach the more modern, mass-market spectrum who enjoy experimenting with New World wines while remaining price and promotion conscious; the younger chardonnay girl who tends to choose white wine for its healthy and social aspects and who is open to experimenting; finally, the adventurer at the premium end of the spectrum is a self-confident drinker who tends to value flavour and New World wines. Even if we might have some doubts about the general applicability of these categories, it is clear that wine drinkers are increasingly fragmented even if there is a pronounced trend in favour of New World wines.

Following a number of social commentators, the *neophilic* search – defined as a desire for variety to compensate anxiety – for new taste sensations, new combinations and mixtures, remains as the dynamic principle of innovation and characterize the *homo culinarius*. As the restaurant is part of the entertainment industry in Westernized societies and is concerned with the marketing of emotions, desires and states of mind (Beardsworth and Keil, 1997), wine drinking appears to be more informal than was historically the case, but more controlled than in any other social context. Unlike the professional wine-taster, the drinker in a restaurant has no other possibility than to swallow his/her wine and the mouth acts as an organ of sensory and sensual experience, and of censorship as well. The sensorial experience is at its peak and the control of emotions and moderate alcohol consumption are an integral part of this social act. Taking possession of certain foods and 'all the manners' involved in their use, grants the individual a certain status, and in the case of wine drinking, most of the time, it is socially unacceptable to become drunk after immoderate wine consumption. Even in restaurants where the informal dominates, wine drinking remains a strong marker of identity and difference where taste is culturally shaped and socially controlled. The wine waiter subdues the diners and establishes boundaries and hierarchies. Wine is ultimately bound up with social relations, including those of power, of inclusion and exclusion, as well as with cultural ideas about classification, the human body and the meaning of health. The importance of taste in the decision to drink wine is therefore the key attitudinal factor in the studies of food and drink choice.

It is undeniable that consumers are becoming better educated in their wine selection and for instance in America, wine consumers have become receptive to wines from all over the world. National prejudices do, however, remain strong elsewhere and it is difficult to ask a French or Italian to drink New World wines. The shaping of tastes is largely defined by the cultural experience of each individual. The choice of wine is influenced by several factors: price, brand, region, vintage year, wine-maker, variety of grape and style, and this array may exceed 50–100 choices in a typical restaurant. The individual profile and the context of the situation all play an important role. It is equally true to say that the degree to which a consumer has existing experience and knowledge of a wine will influence the adoption rate (Dodd, 1997). Traditional European wines will be ranged in this category where a preliminary contact with the product is needed in order to establish a positive appreciation of its taste. New World wines offer a simple and straight forward pleasure as their taste is very often associated with values which fit our modern societies: they are good value, easy to drink and to taste, and offer permanence of stable characteristics. On the other hand, French wines are more complicated due to the rigid and costly French system of *appellations* (AOC), always changing in relation to the vintage and the art of the wine-maker in that particular year, quite expensive and very complex to decrypt. It has to be said that the majority of consumers privilege the New World type of wines as it reduces their anxiety about choices and desires of tastes.

For many restaurants, wine, beer and spirit sales can substantially increase the final bill for the customer and by the same token the total revenue for the restaurant. In addition, the margins on these beverages are frequently higher than food items. It is why the wine list ought to be considered as a major selling technique to increase impulse wine purchases in a restaurants setting (Dodd, 1997). In relation to the choice of wines, it is essential to take into account the variety of wine drinkers with their own and specific cultural knowledge of the product. Various marketing strategies have to be deployed to embrace the wide range of drinkers from the unfamiliar and intimidated individual who needs some help with the purchase of a wine to accompany his/her meal to the knowledgeable and experienced wine drinker who wants to demonstrate his ability to evaluate the product and combine it with the food. The type of restaurants and the way wine is presented either as a wine list or attached to the menu will influence the drinker. It is equally important to make sure that the wine list responds to the wide range of tastes by enabling individuals to find a price and quality level to suit themselves. It is why the training of the staff plays an important role when advising on what to drink. The wine list must also be created in relation to the menu and must reflect changes in the menu. Restaurants are seen as a more ephemeral market and they have to offer greater choice in terms of age and quality of wine than in retail stores. Finally, as wine remains a complex object of distinction, it is necessary to adopt a clear and well-informed discourse when presenting the different wines. Grape variety, country of origin, promotion and brand are among the features required to illustrate the distinction features of the wines. At the end of the day, the consumer is king. To facilitate his/her experience of wine drinking, the restaurant has to ensure that its selection meets the expectations and desires of its customers.

Bibliography

Beardsworth, A. and Keil, T. (1997). *Sociology on the Menu*. London: Routledge.

Bell, D. and Valentine, G. (1997). *Consuming Geographies*. London: Routledge.

Burzynska, J. (2001). Facing forward. *Harpers*. June, p. 38.

Chiva, M. (1985). *Le Doux et L'amer*. Oxford: PUF.

Cousin, J., Foskett, D. and Gillespie, C. (2001). *Food and Beverage Management*, 2nd edition. Harlow: Pearson Education.

Dodd, T. (1997). Factors that influence the adoption and diffusion of new wine products. *Hospitality Research Journal* **20** (3), 123–136.

Dodd, T. (1997). Techniques to increase impulse wine purchases in a restaurant setting. *Journal of Restaurant and Foodservice Marketing* **2** (1), 63–73.

Elias, N. (1978). *The Civilising Process*. Oxford: Basil Blackwell.

Garrier, G. (1995). *Histoire Sociale et Culturelle Du Vin*. Paris: Bordas Culture.

Gillespie, C. (2001). *European Gastronomy in the 21st Century*. Oxford: Butterworth-Heinemann.

Hall, J., Shaw, M. and Doole, I. (1997). Cross-cultural analysis of wine consumption motivations. *International Journal of Wine Marketing* **9** (2/3), 83–92.

Howley, M. and Young, N. (1992). Low-alcohol wines: the consumer's choice? *International Journal of Wine Marketing* **4** (3), 45–56.

Mennell, S. (1987). *All Manners of Food*. Oxford: Basil Blackwell.

Mitchell, V.W. and Greatorex, M. (1989). Risk reducing strategies used in the purchase of wine in the UK. *European Journal of Marketing* **23** (9), 31–46.

Norström, T. (2001). *Alcohol in Postwar Europe: Consumption, Drinking Patterns, Consequences and Policy Responses in 15 European Countries*. Stockholm: European Commission, ECAS.

Puisais, J. 1987. *Le Goût et L'enfant*. Paris: Flammarion.

Smith, D.E. and Solgaard, H.S. (1997). Is there a global convergence in consumer's tastes? *CEMS Business Review* **2**, 73–84.

Thompson, K.E., Haziris, N. and Alekos, P.J. (1994). Attitudes and food choice behaviour. *British Food Journal* **96** (11), 9–13.

Unwin, T. (1991). *Wine and the Vine. An Historical Geography of Viticulture and the Wine Trade*. London: Routledge.

Warde, A. and Marten, L. (2000). *Eating Out*. Cambridge: Cambridge University Press.

Hospitality, Leisure & Tourism Series

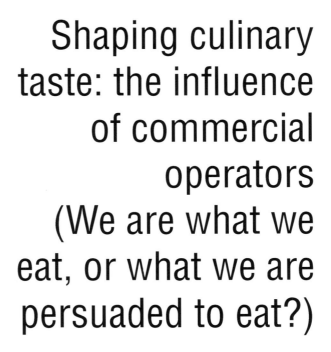

CHAPTER 7

Shaping culinary taste: the influence of commercial operators (We are what we eat, or what we are persuaded to eat?)

Maureen Brookes

Introduction

In many, if not most parts of the world, people are consuming more meals outside of the home than ever before. This increase in consumption has been matched with an increase in restaurant provision ranging from fast food to fine dining establishments. Given the wealth of choice available to consumers, one could argue that to be successful a restaurant must be marketing oriented and offer products and services that satisfy customer needs and wants. Within food and beverage provision, a reasonable assumption might also be that consumer wants are reflective of their culinary taste. Or is it? The industry is full of savvy operators who have conquered both domestic and international markets with standardized branded restaurant concepts. The question therefore arises as to whether these operators have succeeded by shaping consumer demand, and hence taste, through the nature of their provision, or whether they are successful because they deliver menu products in line with consumer taste?

Attempting to answer this question might appear as futile as trying to determine whether it was the chicken or the egg that actually came first. Indeed there are views just as polar on the subject. There are those that believe that the industry is product led and therefore demand is being shaped by provision. For instance, Wood (1996a) argues that:

> There is a growing recognition that, in commercial food and beverage provision, the power of the purveyors of such services has been used quite determinedly to circumscribe the food choice of consumers as well as the variety of foods (dishes, meals) they may choose to consume. (Wood, p. 6)

Alternatively, there are those that believe that the industry is market led and provision is shaped by consumer taste. As Kara et al. (1997) report 'today's menus reflect a marketing oriented approach' (p. 318) and thus restaurateurs must therefore be true to the marketing concept (Kotler et al., 2003). However, there are those that are sceptical (and undoubtedly with good reason) that the restaurant industry possesses any 'pure' marketing oriented firms. Blois (2000) for instance identifies the 'Type B' marketing oriented firm that adopts a customer focus only when market forces require it to (p. 30). Furthermore Gillespie (1994) argues that what determines the actual content of menus is operators' perceptions of consumer tastes and these of course, might not be accurate. In addition, the marketing literature is full of examples of hospitality firms that are clearly more production and sales oriented than they are market oriented.

It would appear therefore that the original question posed is not necessarily an either/or proposition; rather there may be a continuum of possibilities on the demand led vs. supply driven argument. This chapter therefore attempts to provide further insight into the extent to which restaurateurs can shape culinary taste through the nature of their provision. It begins by examining the broader environmental forces that are driving consumer demand for meals outside of the home and identifies two different market segments. Against this background, consumers' criteria for selecting a restaurant are considered in order to identify the importance of the food and beverage component in purchase decisions. The chapter then investigates the nature of restaurant provision in an increasingly competitive environment. It examines the trend towards branded restaurant concepts and the influence of branding on consumer purchase decisions. The argument presented suggests that both social forces and marketing strategies can heavily impact upon consumers' restaurant choice.

Drivers of demand

An investigation of the international restaurant industry reveals that it is growing steadily and making a significant contribution to many domestic economies. In the UK for instance, the value of the dining out market increased by 32 per cent between 1996 and 2001 (Mintel International Group Ltd, 2001) and by June 2002 sales reached £24.78 billion (Paterson, 2003). Over the last year alone, there was a 3.8 per cent increase in the value of the market (Paterson, 2003). A similar trend is apparent in the USA with fast food sales totalling US $135 billion and restaurants and cafes a further US $163.3 billion in 2001 (Euromonitor, 2002a,b). Furthermore, this trend is not restricted to western economies. Various research reports indicate industry growth in Australia and within Asian, European and South American economies. Even in countries suffering from economic recession in the latest period monitored (1997–2001), there was still growth in the fast food sector of the industry. In Germany for instance, Euromonitor (2002c) research indicates a remarkable 49 per cent growth rate in the fast food market over this period.

Hospitality, Leisure & Tourism Series

At the risk of stating the obvious, the increased value of the market is a result of people dining out more frequently although there are diverse levels of consumption reported in different parts of the world. Americans consumed 139 restaurant meals per person per year (Anon, 2000), in the UK over 11 per cent of adults now eat out in the evenings at least once a week (Mintel International Group Ltd, 1999). In Asia, industry reports suggest that eating out in India for instance has increased on average from once a month to twice a week over the last few years (Anon, 2001). This growth in consumption is in turn being driven by a number of other economic and socio-cultural forces. For many nations, it is the increased wealth of the population and the resultant disposable income that enables people to purchase more meals outside of the home. Recent research by Mintel International Group Ltd (2002a) indicates that propensity to eat out increases with affluence; people from the socio-economic group ABs are almost twice as likely to eat out on a monthly basis than those within the E grouping. In many countries, such as the UK, the proportion of ABs is growing throughout the population. Personal disposable income is also reported to be on the rise in South Korea and thus driving the demand for fast food operations (Lee and Ulgado, 1997). In other countries there are pockets of affluence. For instance, while there is disparity in income levels in China, Euromonitor (2002d) reports that increased disposable income in urban populations is a key force driving restaurant demand. Similar patterns are also reported elsewhere across the globe.

There are of course other contributory factors. In some parts of the world (in many countries in Europe and within North America for instance) the average age of the population is increasing. As the post World War II baby boomers reach retirement, they have more leisure time on their hands as well as greater levels of disposable income and therefore more opportunity to dine out. In China, the one child policy is reported to be a driving force in the stimulation of the fast food industry in particular (Euromonitor, 2002d) as it has enabled and encouraged parents to spend more on their child. In the Philippines, Lui and Chen (2000) advise that the student population is responsible for growth in eating out markets, particularly within the fast food sector. The socio-cultural trends that see a greater number of single households and single parent households continue to play critical roles in the dining out process (Frumkin, 1997). In addition, where women have become a more integral part of the workforce and there are a greater percentage of working couples, time constraints become a determinant in the decision to eat away from home (Mawson and Fearne, 1996).

In many parts of the world, people perceive themselves to be 'cash rich but time poor' and dine away from home more often as a result. This particular socio-cultural force has been largely responsible for the rapid growth of the 'home meal replacement' sector of the industry in countries like Canada, the USA and the UK (see for instance Mintel International Group Ltd, 2002b; Browne, 2003). In the USA alone, 6.5 billion meals are purchased each year in restaurants and taken home to eat (Krummert, 1997). While take-away restaurants are well established in many countries and cultures, time pressures in many societies have more recently resulted in the creation of the 'grab and go' consumer (Perlik, 2002), who partakes in an activity delicately referred to as a 'cruise chews'. While not all consumers like to eat on the go, time constraints and price considerations have made the 'take out to eat in' option attractive for many consumers. While this market sector is relevant to this debate, the remainder of the chapter will focus on meals consumed outside of the home within commercial establishments.

It is necessary to examine these broad demand drivers in order to better understand why consumers are dining out and therefore what they are seeking from their meal experience. According to Beardsworth and Keil (1997) people have been choosing to dine out for leisure purposes rather than necessity-sake since the time of the T'ang Dynasty. In China today socialization remains firmly embedded in the act of dining out as it is not a cultural norm to hold dinner parties in the home (Euromonitor, 2002e). In these instances the meal purchase is reflective of 'a primary investment by the consumer in the act of dining out for dining out's sake' (Wood, 1996, p. 13). This type of dining is often linked to special occasions (see for instance, Lui and Chen's report on the Philippines, 2000), but increasing affluence in some parts of the world has resulted in

Hospitality, Leisure & Tourism Series

dining out becoming more commonplace (Mintel International Group Ltd, 2002a).

However, as the socio-cultural forces discussed above indicate, consumers also purchase meals from restaurants for the sake of convenience. 'Time poverty' is a driver for the increased demand for meals within commercial establishments at lunchtime (Perlik, 2002). Most people need sustenance during the day and many consumers perceive it to be more convenient to eat out in a commercial establishment during the lunch break than to prepare and pack a lunch. Wood (1996) argues that around a quarter of all meals served in the hospitality industry have been purchased as an ancillary activity rather than an activity in its own right. For instance, the purchase of meals in commercial establishments is frequently a secondary activity when people are shopping or undertaking some other leisure pursuit and find themselves hungry. Wood (1996) suggests that when the purchase of a meal is not the primary activity people are 'eating out', rather than 'dining out'. Numerous others support Wood's argument and there is a growing recognition of a distinction between the eating out and dining out sectors of the industry.

By definition, these two sectors are distinguished by the relative importance of the eating experience to the consumer and as such it is likely that the criteria consumers use to select a restaurant also differs. More importantly, the relative importance of the actual menu on offer, and the extent to which it is reflective of consumers' culinary taste, may also vary between these sectors. The following section explores how consumers make purchase decisions; first generally and then within the context of the eating out and dining out markets.

Consumer purchase decisions

It is well recognized in marketing literature that consumers proceed through a series of stages when making purchases. The process is triggered by the recognition of unsatisfied needs. Consumers then seek out information about alternatives offers, evaluate these alternatives against certain criteria, make a decision about what to buy and then evaluate their decision post purchase (see, e.g. Solomon and Stuart, 2003). Whether consumers go through all of these stages and the time spent on any of these stages is dependent upon the risk or value of the purchase, or whether it is a high or low involvement purchase (Pickton and Broderick, 2001). Whereas consumers might be highly involved in the decision of where to dine for a special occasion, popping out to buy a sandwich for lunch is a low involvement purchase. Consumers might be less likely therefore to spend as much time on deciding where to eat out than where to dine out.

Understanding particular purchase criteria in restaurant selection therefore becomes important in determining the extent to which restaurateurs can influence consumer choice and hence culinary taste. According to Marketing Guru Philip Kotler consumers purchase 'bundles of benefits' with varying abilities to satisfy their needs (Kotler et al., p. 205). Restaurants in particular have been described and conceptualized by many marketers as a product package where food and beverage is potentially only one small element. If consumers perceive an eating or dining out experience as a benefit bundle, they are likely to use multiple criteria when making purchase decisions, especially with high involvement purchases.

Hollenson (2003) divides these consumer choice criteria into four broad categories: cost, performance, social and availability attributes (p. 121). Potential restaurant customers could consider purchase price or average cost of the meal in the first category, performance in terms of quality of the food and beverage or its taste in the second, reputation of a restaurant or its image in the third, and location or accessibility in the final category. Therefore, if consumers were selecting particular restaurants on the basis of whether the menu is reflective of their culinary taste, they would prioritize performance attributes in their selection criteria. However, which categories of criteria are most important to individual consumers, and which criteria would be considered most important within each category is also dependent upon a number of other cultural, social, personal and psychological influences (Dibb et al., 1997).

Isolating and prioritizing consumer selection criteria is therefore not a simple task, especially in the restaurant industry. Research undertaken by Kivela (1997) in Hong Kong suggests that customer choice variables in restaurant selection differed according to restaurant type, dining out occasion, age and occupation. Auty's (1992) research also suggests that meal occasion impacts upon the selection criteria used and hence consumers may apply different criteria when choosing where to 'eat out' than where to 'dine out'. Kivela (1997) concluded from his research that it is potentially unimportant criteria (or purchase attributes) that can determine customers' final restaurant choice. In other words, even if a menu at a particular restaurant is more reflective of a potential customer's taste, that customer may still opt for another restaurant on the basis of cost, social or availability attributes. These findings beg the question therefore of how important the 'food and beverage' component is for consumers in a restaurant's benefit bundle.

Choosing where to dine out

Unfortunately, there does not appear to be a clear-cut answer to this question and research findings are quite varied. Clark and Wood (1999) found in their research of people in the UK who 'dine out' frequently that 'quality of food' and 'range of food' are important considerations and that these criteria are also determinants of customer loyalty. The authors however point out that 'quality' of food offers a range of interpretations. Mintel International Group Ltd (2002a) research suggests that consumers define quality by the ingredients used to prepare menu options for two reasons. Firstly, as a result of the more recent external environmental forces that have raised consumer fears about food safety and secondly, as a result of consumers generally becoming more health conscious (see for instance Paterson, 2003). Silver (2001) reports that diners are demanding local or regional cuisine in order to trace the origins of ingredients. Mintel International Group Ltd (2001) findings support those of Silver and further suggest that consumers want vegetarian meals in restaurants even when they are not vegetarian due to their food safety concerns.[1]

Food choice, or range of food items on offer, has also been determined to be an important purchase attribute for restaurant consumers. Mintel International Group Ltd (2002a) reports that customers in the UK look specifically for 'a wide menu choice' for the simple reasons that they like to try different dishes. Research conducted within the Philippines (Lui and Chen, 2000) and the USA by the San Francisco Convention and Visitors Bureau suggests that diners in these countries also like to try something new or not available at home and furthermore that many prefer to dine in new restaurants. In dining out experiences however, whether or not at new restaurants, service quality is also deemed an important purchase criterion (see for instance Mintel International Group Ltd, 2002b).

These research findings suggest that the food and beverage component is clearly an important benefit within the bundle provided by the 'dining out' experience. Although Clark and Wood (1999) question the concept of the meal experience as a 'holistic abstraction', they argue that tangible (e.g. food and beverage) rather than intangible factors are of greater importance in consumer loyalty. The authors further argue that the additional elements of the meal experience (the bundle of other purchase attributes) only become important if the central tangible aspect of dining out (e.g. food and beverage) is acceptable to the consumer. The research reviewed here also reveals that when dining out, greater emphasis is placed upon performance attributes such as food quality in the purchase criteria. However, what is not identified through the research undertaken is the extent to which quality is defined or judged by the food's ability to reflect consumer taste.

Given the reported findings on menu selection, some light is also shed on the extent to which restaurant provision is driven by consumer taste. Consumers are clearly demanding organic and healthy choice options on menus and a few restaurateurs are making an effort to meet this demand. While it could be argued that menu provision is to some extent at least, consumer driven, in reality these restaurants are few and far between. In addition, the research suggests that other external environmental forces related to food safety, rather than customer taste, are driving this particular customer demand.

Furthermore, as consumers want to try new menu dishes and even new restaurants, there is clearly the opportunity for a product driven approach within this market sector. The increasing popularity of celebrity chefs and their proprietary restaurants facilitates further scope to influence consumer taste. Mennel (1985) notes particular reasons that chefs who have control of the menu are able to shape culinary provision within the commercial sector. Within the marketing literature, celebrity chefs are often considered product rather than consumer oriented (see for instance Bowie and Buttle, 2003). In addition, a recognized pattern within the industry is that food trends or fashions which become embedded in the fine dining sector eventually emerge in family restaurants, then fast food, and ultimately to home meal replacements and dishes being cooked within the home (Holt, 1998). This tendency was particularly noted within ethnic cuisine and consumer preferences for more exotic flavours. Sperber (2001) argues that by the time food trends reach the fast food sector they are catering to mainstream tastes. In other words a chef may start to experiment with new ingredients to create new menu choices, consumers choose these menu items for their newness (or alternatively for image reasons as discussed below) and eventually these dishes and their rapidly developed competitor versions become more and more accepted among diners until they become embedded in mainstream tastes. Consequently, this pattern of adoption suggests that restaurateurs do indeed influence culinary taste in the dining out market segment.

Choosing where to eat out

Research undertaken in the eating out market sector also identifies a number of different purchase criteria used by consumers. Frumkin (1997) suggests that consumer attitudes to restaurant selection over the next 10–15 years will follow the same general patterns as those tracked in the 1980s and 1990s. Customers will look for 'value, convenience, menu variety, healthful choices, fun atmosphere and a family-friendly attitude' (p. 74). Wilkerson (1999) also reports that consumers seek good value, convenience, greater variety, super service and higher quality.

The research findings within this market sector indicate that cost and availability attributes are distinctly more important than performance attributes for consumers. The purchase criterion of value clearly falls within the cost category. While value is recognized within the marketing literature as a function of both price and quality (see for instance Lovelock et al.,

Hospitality, Leisure & Tourism Series

1996), it is purported that price is becoming a more important consideration given higher levels of perceived quality when 'eating out'. Lee and Ulgado (1997) also report on their research into fast food establishments in the USA and Korea that the more ingrained fast food becomes in a culture, the greater the importance of price, especially as a promotional tool.

The relative importance of convenience and speed of service can almost certainly be attributed to the environmental forces stimulating time poverty, whether real or perceived. The significance of the food and beverage component of the eating out benefit bundle appears to be less in this sector therefore than the dining out sector. As a result, there is yet more scope for commercial operators to adopt a product led approach to menu design and therefore to influence culinary taste, particularly as the research identifies that menu variety is also an important purchase attribute within this sector.

The arguments presented thus far suggest that current environmental trends are shaping the nature of consumer demand within both dining out and eating out market sectors. Performance attributes and the actual food and beverage element of the meal experience appear to be of greater importance in customer purchase decisions in the dining out market. Nonetheless, within both dining out and eating out sectors the potential for commercial operators to adopt a product oriented approach and thus influence consumer taste has been clearly identified. However, it is also important to consider the nature of restaurant provision in light of these arguments in order to further determine the extent to which restaurateurs can shape culinary taste.

The nature of provision

Not surprisingly, there has been a change in the nature of restaurant provision in response to greater consumer demand. Not only is there an increase in the number of restaurants, but also in the variety of restaurants available. In some parts of the world, other environmental forces have also had an impact on the nature of restaurant provision. For instance in China, the recent introduction of simpler licensing procedures has encouraged the development of the fast food sector of the market (Euromonitor, 2002d). This is rather different than the growth of this sector in the Philippines reported above, where growth has been a result of demand created by a growing student population.

Expansion in commercial provision has in turn created an increasingly competitive marketplace particularly in the mid-market and fast food sectors. In addition, there is growing competition reported between mid-market operations like family and quick service restaurants with fast food operators (Perlik, 2002). In the USA for instance, McDonald's is now experimenting with table service and a wider menu selection to better compete with quick service restaurants for market share. Consolidation within the industry has also enabled commercial operators to gain market share, although levels of consolidation are variable in different parts of the world (Euromonitor, 2002a). Restaurateurs have also tried to gain competitive advantage by differentiating their offering from that of the competition, in a way that adds value to the consumer, whether or not this value is real or perceived. Both consolidation and the need for differentiation have in turn led to greater development of branded restaurant concepts.

While branding began in this industry back in the 1980s with high street restaurants, the trend has spread to contract catering firms as well as to restaurant provision in hotels. For instance Silver (2001) reports on the growing trend for hotel companies to develop restaurant brands for system-wide roll-out in order to remain competitive. Celebrity chefs and their propriety restaurants have also been likened to branded products (Mintel International Group Ltd, 2002b).

A brand can be defined as

> a name, a term, a symbol or any other unique element of a product that identifies one firm's product(s) and sets them apart from the competition. (Solomon and Stuart, 2003)

Theoretically a brand offers a number of benefits to both the commercial operator and the consumer. For producers of brands, it is argued that brands create customer loyalty, thereby allowing firms not only to maintain a strong market share but also to increase profitability (Blois, 2000). In an increasingly competitive environment therefore, brands make strong commercial sense for restaurant operators.

For consumers, the brand is purported to decrease purchase risk. Wells and Prensky (1996) identify five types of perceived risk: functional, physical, financial, social and psychological (p. 272). Brands reduce the functional, physical and financial risks by clearly identifying to consumers product or functional attributes of the brand as well as the benefits they provide (Kotler et al., 2001). As discussed earlier in this chapter, people buy benefits not product attributes, although these may be delivered by the product attributes. For instance, in the restaurant industry, customers buy convenience, not the actual restaurant location. A well-defined brand therefore signifies the benefits offered to consumers and these can be readily assessed against their specific purchase criteria. In a crowded marketplace, brands therefore also make sense to consumers as they simplify purchase decisions.

Brands reduce social and psychological purchase risks through their personality and values that they symbolize (Kotler et al., 2001). Elliott (1997) argues that people are consumers of the symbolic meaning of products and these are portrayed by their images. For instance, the Hard Rock Café has a fundamentally different personality or image than Burger King, yet consumers could dine on hamburgers in either branded restaurant. It was suggested earlier in this chapter that image, as a social purchase attribute, may have a role to play in consumers' dining out decisions. This symbolic meaning is often communicated through the consumption of brands (Jamal and Goode, 2001). In other words, consumers select brands they perceive to have the appropriate social or psychological image.

Gottdeiner (1985) suggests that the impact of brand symbolism depends on the interrelationship between a brand's image (e.g. as defined by its personality and values) and the consumer's self-image. Self-image can be described quite simply as the view an individual has of his or her own personality (Wells and Prensky, 1996, p. 182). However, the authors distinguish between consumer's actual self-image (e.g. the personality they have) and their ideal self-image (the personality they strive to be). In brand purchase decisions, consumers select brands according to the congruence between the brand image and either their actual or ideal self-image. Which of these they use as a reference point can depend upon the particular purchase occasion (Aaker, 1999). In the dining out market, a consumer may choose the restaurant of a celebrity chef if dining out with a person he or she would like to impress. In this instance, the image of the restaurant selected would appeal to the consumer's ideal self-image. When dining on his or her own or with a different peer group, that person may choose a restaurant more reflective of their actual self-image. These scenarios clearly indicate that perceived social and psychological risks could alter the values that customers hold important and thus influence consumer purchase decisions by impacting upon the relative importance of different purchase criteria. As Goldsmith et al. (1997) report 'reflecting desired end states or ways of living, values may in part represent some of the fundamental motives that drive and direct consumer behaviour' (p. 352).

Wright et al. (2000a) sum up these arguments by suggesting that one way of thinking about brands 'is to identify the benefits and symbolic values with which consumers associate it and how these values and benefits affect its appeal relative to the competition' (p. 432). Branding is therefore a way for commercial operators to influence consumer purchase behaviour. More importantly to the topic under investigation is that branding is reported to influence consumer perceptions of taste. Wright et al. (2000b) argue that consumer perception of the taste of food is a psychological construction based on gustatory properties of the food itself as well as the expectations generated by marketing stimuli, such as the brand name.

Furthermore, Sirgy et al. (1997) found that self-image congruity with branded products is a strong predictor of customer satisfaction. Graeff (1996) concluded that consumers' evaluations of publicly consumed brands were more affected by the congruence between brand image and ideal self-image than actual self-image. In the restaurant industry therefore, consumers could select brands on the basis of perceived congruence with their ideal self-image and thus the food itself will be of secondary importance to image or social purchase attributes (Mintel International Group Ltd, 2002a). If their dining experience lives up to their expectations of their ideal self, they are not only more likely to return but also to recommend the restaurant to their friends (Kotler et al., 2003) thus perpetuating the importance of image and social purchase attributes. Branded restaurant concepts therefore further increase the potential for commercial operators to influence culinary tastes.

However, Mintel International Group Ltd. (2002a) reports that brands can only engender loyalty if they continually evolve. Consumers are reported to have become increasingly fickle and as a result, branded operators have looked at different ways of entertaining customers to increase the perceived value of their dining or eating experience. The outcome has been widespread growth in the provision of dining venues that combine food with some sort of entertainment. There has also been extensive global development of the themed restaurant or pub, where food, beverage, decor and entertainment are reflective of a particular theme. For instance recent *Key Note* research (1999) identified 3000 themed pubs within the UK alone. While themes are variable, such as sports, music or television programmes, Brown and Patterson (2000) report that country themed operations are the most abundant and in particular Irish themed establishments. The latter have sprung up as far afield as the USA, Japan, Korea, and even in Italy, which does not even have a national pub culture (Brown and Patterson, 2000).

The added value of these themed operations is the provision of the complete national experience and Brown and Patterson (2000) question whether this branded experience is perceived to be better than the real thing in today's postmodern society. For instance, consumers can experience India in Las Vegas without the threat of dysentery. Apparently the value that consumers place upon the perceived authentic national experience is so great that the authors report there are even replica Irish pubs springing up in Dublin, Cork and other cities of Ireland at the expense of independent pub. Given the current political forces raising consumer fears about the safety of travelling, there is enormous potential for further growth of the country themed dining venue. This perceived added value provided by these types of dining venues could further diminish the importance of the meal component if the dining or eating out benefit bundle. As Wood (1996) argues, marketing has emphasized

Hospitality, Leisure & Tourism Series

dining out as theatre and this emphasis on dining as a holistic experience has further reduced the importance of food and beverage in the experience. As a result, commercial operators are given even greater opportunity to influence consumer restaurant choice and hence taste.

We are what we eat, or what we are persuaded to eat?

As far back as 1996, Wood reported that one of the 'least understood factors influencing contemporary diet is the ability of corporate powers to shape food tastes' (p. 12). This chapter has sought to shed some light on this issue by examining both demand and supply drivers within the commercial restaurant industry. What has clearly been revealed by this examination is the distinct potential that restaurateurs have to shape culinary taste as a result of the forces driving consumer demand and the forces influencing the nature of restaurant provision.

As the chapter identifies, consumers across the globe are dining out more frequently and this in itself creates an opportunity for commercial operators to influence taste. The broader macro-environmental forces examined suggest this trend towards greater meal consumption outside of the home is not only based on financial ability but other socio-cultural forces as well. As a result, two distinct market sectors, dining out and eating out, can be identified and differentiated by the relative importance of the food and beverage in consumer purchase decisions.

The research reviewed within the chapter suggests that in the dining out market, where meal consumption is a primary activity, performance attributes heavily influence consumer purchase decisions. Both food quality and menu variety are deemed important purchase attributes, however food quality does not necessarily reflect the taste of the food per se. In addition, consumer desire to try new dishes and restaurants creates further opportunity to shape consumer taste. In the eating out market, cost and availability attributes clearly outweigh performance attributes in purchase decisions, thereby giving commercial operators even greater potential to influence consumer taste.

On the supply side of the equation, the increasingly competitive marketplace has fuelled the trend towards branded restaurant concepts. As the chapter revealed, brands reduce purchase risks for consumers especially when faced with an overwhelming choice of restaurants. As brands can also symbolize a consumer's ideal self-image, consumers are more likely to be influenced by image purchase attributes. Furthermore, in an effort to evolve and add value to the dining experience, branded commercial operators now provide even more holistic experiences combining food, beverage and entertainment. This growing trend further diminishes the relative importance of the actual food and beverage component of the meal experience and thus provides additional opportunity for restaurateurs to influence consumer taste.

Wood (1996) argues that if the food is of diminishing importance in the restaurant purchase decision, then it is a result of the way in which dining out has been promoted and marketed. The arguments presented in this chapter clearly support this proposition but indicate that socio-cultural forces also have an influential role. This chapter also supports the proposition of that taste can be coloured by expectations generated by marketing. There is clearly ample potential for commercial operators to shape consumer taste, particularly in branded restaurants. Perhaps, after all, you can lead a horse to water and make it drink as well as eat?

End note

1 A survey conducted in the UK in 2001 revealed that 28 per cent of respondents opt for vegetarian meals when eating out although only 3 per cent claim to be true vegetarians.

Bibliography

Aaker, J. (1999). The malleable self: the role of self-expression in persuasion. *Journal of Marketing Research* **36** (1), 45–57.

Anon (2000). Eating out is really in. *Prepared Foods* **169** (3), 3.

Anon (2001). Eating out is in. *Business India* Downloaded from http://get_xmal.asp?booleanTerm=%28restaurant%20 AND%20trends on 2 June 2002.

Auty, S. (1992). Consumer choice and segmentation in the restaurant industry. *The Service Industries Journal* **12** (3), 324–339.

Beardsworth, A. and Keil, T. (1997). *Sociology on the Menu London*. London: Routledge.

Blois, K. (2000). *The Oxford Textbook of Marketing*. Oxford: Oxford University Press.

Bowie, D. and Buttle, F. (2003). *Hospitality Marketing*. Oxford: Butterworth-Heinemann.

Brown, S. and Patterson, A. (2000). Knick-knack paddy-whack, give a pub a theme. *Journal of Marketing Management* **16**, 647–662.

Browne, A. (2003). Britain is the ready-meal glutton of Europe. *The Times* 21 February, p. 3.

Clark, M. and Wood, R. (1999). Consumer loyalty in the restaurant industry – a preliminary exploration of the issues. *International Journal of Contemporary Hospitality Management* **10** (4), 139–144.

Dibb, S., Simkin, L, Pride, W.M. and Ferrell, O.C. (1997). *Marketing Concepts and Strategies*, 3rd European edition, Boston: Houghton Mifflin.

Elliott, R. (1997). Existential consumption and irrational desire. *European Journal of Marketing* **31** (3/4), 285–296.

Euromonitor (2002a). Fast food in the USA. Downloaded from http://www.euromonitor.com/mrm/default.asp on 14 October 2002.

Euromonitor (2002b). Restaurants and cafes in the USA. Downloaded from http://www.euromonitor.com/mrm/default.asp on 15 October 2002.

Euromonitor (2002c). Fast food in Germany. Downloaded from http://www.euromonitor.com/mrm/default.asp on 14 October 2002.

Euromonitor (2002d). Fast food in China. Downloaded from http://www.euromonitor.com/mrm/default.asp on 14 October 2002.

Euromonitor (2002e). Restaurants and cafes in China. Downloaded from http://www.euromonitor.com/mrm/default. asp on 14 October 2002.

Frumkin, P. (1997). Tomorrow's customer: a look at the future. *Nation's Restaurant News* **31** (43), 74.

Gillespie, C. (1994). Gastrosophy and nouvelle cuisine: entrepreneurial fashion and fiction. *British Food Journal* **96** (10), 19–23.

Goldsmith, R., Frieden, J. and Henderson, K. (1997). The impact of social values on food-related attitudes. *British Food Journal* **99** (9), 352–357.

Gottdeiner, M. (1985). Hegemony and mass culture: a semiotic approach. *American Journal of Sociology* **90** (Fall), 979–1001.

Graeff, T. (1996). Using promotional messages to manage the effects of brand and self-image on brand evaluations. *Journal of Consumer Marketing* **13** (3), 4–18.

Hollenson, S. (2003). *Global Marketing A Market-Responsive Approach*, 2nd Edition. Oxford: Pearson Education Ltd.

Holt, D. (1998). Does cultural capital structure American consumption? *Journal of Consumer Research* **25**, 1–25.

Jamal, A. and Goode, M. (2001). Consumers and brands: a study of the impact of self-image congruence on brand preference and satisfaction. *Marketing Intelligence and Planning* **19** (7), 482–492.

Kara, A., Kaynak, E. and Kucukemiroglu, O. (1997). Marketing strategies for fast-food restaurants: a customer view. *British Food Journal* **99** (9), 318–324.

Kivela, J.J. (1997). Restaurant marketing: selection and segmentation in Hong Kong. *International Journal of Contemporary Hospitality Management* **9** (3), 116–123.

Kotler, P., Armstrong, G., Saunders, J. and Wong, V. (2001). *Principles of Marketing*, 3rd European edition. Oxford: Pearson Education Ltd.

Kotler, P., Bowens, J. and Makens, J. (2003). *Marketing for Hospitality and Tourism*, 3rd International edition. Oxford: Pearson Education Inc.

Krummert, B. (1997). Trends redefine foodservice value. *The Voice of Foodservice Distribution* **33** (12), 41.

Lee, M. and Ulgado, F.M. (1997). Consumer evaluations of fast-food services: a cross national comparison. *Journal of Services Marketing* **11** (1), 39–52.

Lovelock, C., Vandermerwe, S. and Lewis, B. (1996). *Services Marketing*. London: Prentice Hall Europe.

Lui, Chu-Mei and Chen, Kuang-Jung (2000). A look at fastfood competition in the Philippines. *British Food Journal* **102** (2), 122–133.

Mawson, E. and Fearne, A. (1996). Purchasing strategies and decision-making processes in the food service industry: a

Hospitality, Leisure & Tourism Series

case study of UK restaurant chains. *Supply Chain Management* **1** (3), 34–41.

Mennel, S. (1985). *All Manners of Food: Eating and Taste in England and France from the Middle Ages to the Present*. Blackwell.

Mintel International Group Ltd (1999). *Eating Out – Ten Year Trends*. November, Mintel Publications.

Mintel International Group Ltd (2002a). *Restaurants*. April, Mintel Publications.

Mintel International Group Ltd (2002b). *Eating Out Habits*. April, Mintel Publications.

Mintel International Group Ltd (2001). *Eating Out Review*. June, Mintel Publications.

Paterson, L. (2003). The shopping boom that just isn't spent. *The Times*, 1 February, 50–51.

Pedraja, M. and Yague, J. (2001). What information do customers use when choosing a restaurant? *International Journal of Contemporary Hospitality Management* **13** (6), 316–318.

Perlik, A. (2002). Out for lunch. *Restaurants and Institutions* **112** (8), 51–57.

Pickton, D. and Broderick, A. (2001). *Integrated Marketing Communications*. Harlow: Prentice Hall, Inc.

Silver, D. (2001). Breaking with tradition. *Restaurants and Institutions*. **110** (29), 46.

Sirgy, M., Grewal, D., Mangleburg, T., Park, J., Chon, K., Claiborne, C., Johar, J. and Berkman, H. (1997). Assessing the predictive validity of two methods of measuring self-image congruence. *Journal of the Academy of Marketing Science* **25** (3), 229–241.

Solomon, M. and Stuart, E. (2003). *Marketing Real People Real Choices*, 3rd Edition. Harlow: Prentice Hall.

Sperber, B. (2001). Big chains seek a dash of flavor, humility, as dining options grow. *Brandweek* **42** (22), 14.

Wells, W. and Prensky, D. (1996). *Consumer Behaviour*. London: John Wiley and Sons.

Wilkerson, J. (1999). Food franchising trend: consumer preferences power chain operators into the 21st century. *Nations Restaurant News* **33** (24), 28.

Wood, R.C. (1995). *The Sociology of the Meal*. Edinburgh: Edinburgh University Press.

Wood, R.C. (1996a). Talking to themselves: food commentators, food snobbery and market reality. *British Food Journal* **98** (10), 5–11.

Wood, R.C. (1996b). Dining out on sociological neglect. *British Food Journal* **96** (10), 10–14.

Wright, L., Nancarrow, C. and Brace, I. (2000a). Researching taste: layers of analysis. *British Food Journal* **102** (5/6), 429–440.

Wright, L., Nancarrow, C. and Kwok, P (2000b). Food taste preferences and cultural influences on consumption. *British Food Journal* **103** (5), 348–357.

Hospitality, Leisure & Tourism Series

Gender and culinary taste

Roy C. Wood

Any examination of the relationships between gender and culinary taste (and especially women's food tastes) in the public arena of dining, faces two distinct problems. First, there is comparatively little research on the topic. Second, any adequate conceptual framework for investigating the topic is necessarily dependent on understanding something of the development of the sociology of food and eating as a distinctive field of inquiry. In practice, this means focusing on a body of literature characterized by the study of the nature of meals and meal taking in an emphatically *domestic* context. In this chapter, an effort will be made to 'mine' this literature for appropriate concepts, linking these to the limited available research information and some informed speculation on gendered differences in taste in public dining.

Gender and domestic dining

Meals can demonstrate the nature of status differences and relationships in society. The distribution of food as a means of articulating social status is common in many societies. In their seminal collection of social anthropological essays, Jerome, et al. (1980) and their various contributors offer many examples of how in tribal, agricultural and otherwise non-industrial communities, women are disadvantaged in terms of access to food. One of the collection's most memorable observations is contained in a paper by Rosenberg (1980, p. 184) who reports Simoons' (1967) comments on the skinning, cutting up and preparation of reindeer for eating by women of the Siberian Chukchee tribe. In return for this service Chukchee women receive leftovers and bones once men have selected and consumed the choice cuts of meat. This distributive policy is encapsulated in a Chukchee saying – 'being woman, eat crumbs'.

Gender inequalities in food relationships are no less evident in industrial societies. Within the family, status and power differences according to gender can be reflected in the distribution of food. Kerr and Charles (1986) found that very high consumption of meat was almost totally confined to men while very low meat consumption was associated primarily with women and children. Social class differences were important here, with professional/management males consuming less meat than others and manual unskilled workers evidencing the highest consumption. Several other studies have shown that women often give priority to male preferences at the expense of their own, and sometimes even go without food, particularly in families where there is financial hardship.

These status differences tend to be focused through notions of what constitutes 'appropriate' role performance expectations for women and men. In terms of the analysis of gendered food relationships, a critically important study here is that of Murcott (1982) on the social significance of the cooked dinner among Welsh working-class families. Murcott's (1982) achievement was to focus on both the structure of meals and the relationship of these structures to male/female relationships. She found that central to positive perceptions of general family health and well-being was the 'cooked dinner' comprising meat, potatoes, at least one additional vegetable and gravy. Structurally, the cooked dinner was thought of as a meal in itself, and in its proper form was heavy, hot, savoury and generous in size. Meat had to be fresh, fish was not acceptable for the meal to be regarded as proper. Although a succession of courses in a meal was permissible, the cooked dinner could stand as a meal in its own right.

According to Murcott, a symbolically important feature of cooked dinners is the extent to which their preparation validates women's roles in the marital context. There may be some parallel sharing of responsibilities in meal preparation but where this does occur, the male adult is normally construed as simply helping. Women's responsibility for the cooked dinner extends beyond cooking itself to include the process of accommodating family food preferences, especially those of the husband or male partner which invariably take priority. A woman's ability to produce a cooked dinner validates her socially and economically. In Murcott's words:

> If a job defines how a man occupies his time during the working day, to which the wage packet provides regular testimony, proper provision of a cooked dinner testifies that the woman has spent her time in correspondingly suitable fashion ... the cooked dinner in the end symbolizes the home itself, a man's relation to that home and a woman's place in it. (Murcott, 1982, p. 693)

Women's complex relationship with food

Murcott thus links food and eating to the pattern of power relationships within the family and these are essentially gender relationships. Since Murcott's study, a large number of similar, domestically oriented studies have appeared (see Wood, 1995, for commentaries on many of these). The key issues arising from this body of work may be summarized as follows.

- Women's relationship with food is problematic. Most women choose what food is purchased for family consumption (Kerr and Charles, 1986, found this was true in 85 per cent of their cases) but this is often considered a burden rather than a power to determine the domestic dietary cycle. This is because of the need to balance a range of considerations: family tastes and preferences, food cost, variety and nutritional values among them. Women frequently subordinate their own food preferences to those of male partners who are more often than not regarded as unadventurous – though not necessarily fussy-eaters.

- While the vast majority of studies of meals have been undertaken among traditional British working-class or American 'blue collar' families, Charles and Kerr's (1988) work indicates the cooked dinner type meal is certainly common in the British middle-class dietary system. Women's responsibility for the cooked dinner appears to be socially generalized. The cooked dinner is significant across social class and the role of women in the preparation of meals is also widespread.

- Women continue to be the main cooks in most households. The 'absence' of cooked dinners or a female to cook for men can disrupt the (male) social fabric. Ellis (1983) observes that the centrality of food in marital relationships can often lead to violence when men perceive women as in some way failing in the performance of those tasks which are regarded as properly theirs, especially the preparation of meals. Coxon (1983) studied a male cookery class and observed that men only usually learn domestic cooking and have to practise that skill when they have no woman to cook for them. The students Coxon observed contained many absolute beginners who had found themselves womanless through being widowed, divorced or having lost the female relative who cooked for them (e.g. their mother or sister).

Myths of greater democracy

One of the most frequently vaunted 'commonsense' objections to studies of women's roles in food purchase and preparation is that greater marital democracy means that men now play a larger role in these activities than would be suggested by the preceding commentary. This argument is always current, and its history is considered expertly by Mennell et al. (1992). In her study, Dare noted that:

> The mean time per meal … reveals quite starkly the unequal division of labour and the way convenience foods may play a role in reducing women's work time. Breakfasts and snacks are meals featuring a high

> proportion of convenience foods, where time is some-
> what less unequally divided between family members,
> suggesting such meals are prepared by household
> members other than the woman. Yet other meals reveal
> the same high proportion of convenience foods used
> with a grossly unequal division of time. Indeed in prepar-
> ing Sunday lunch women spend 14 times longer than
> men and children combined. (Dare, 1988, pp. 149–150)

A 1993 study by the Mintel Market Research Organization (see e.g. Erlichman, 1993, p. 6) found that around 85 per cent of working women said they were entirely responsible for cooking their household's main meal, a point at least partly supported by Warde and Martens (2000). The brutal truth is that even where male and female partners are in paid work, responsibility for food preparation tends to fall to women. There is evidence of social class variation in this phenomenon. Charles and Kerr (1988, p. 176) found a significant class variation in the gendered division of domestic labour. In both shopping and cooking, Charles and Kerr note, 'men in classes I and II were much more likely to help out with these tasks than their working-class counterparts'. The term 'help out' may be significant in this context as it lends support to the notion that where men are involved in food preparation, it is in an ancillary way, a view also partially recognized by Warde and Martens (2000).

Gendered food tastes and preferences

As noted in the introductory remarks to this chapter, remarkably little is known about women's food tastes. The problem is actually worse than that. Our knowledge of gendered food tastes in general is fairly limited and, for the most part, based on inferences drawn from studies like those reviewed above. Although concepts of taste exist implicitly in much of the sociological literature on food (and sometimes explicitly, see e.g. Bourdieu, 1984; Finkelstein, 1989) there has been little in the way of explicit reflections on the meanings of 'taste' in a culinary context. In part, there is a suspicion that this is because food specifically, and consumption in general, are not yet seen as 'comfortable' or legitimate subjects for sociological analysis (Warde and Martens, 2000, pp. 163–168). This contrasts, for example, with sociological and other disciplinary analyses of 'art' (a not altogether spurious comparison given the frequent allusions to food and cooking as an art form, see Wood, 2000) where the concept of 'taste' is central to an understanding of the social production and consumption of art.

Most sociological discussions of taste embody as a key referent (however implicitly) a hierarchical ordering of taste produced according to social relations of 'class'. Even post-structuralist and postmodernist perspectives with their emphasis on consumption as a phenomenon characterized by the circulation of signs and signifiers rely, however reluctantly, on some notion of the stratification of taste according to socio-economic class. Away from the opaqueness of these postmodernist commentaries, Bourdieu's (1984) seminal work on French 'tastes' attempted a fusion of neo-Marxist and structuralist analysis centred on notions of 'cultural capital' in taste (refer to Chapter 1 for a detailed exposition of Bourdieu's work). Bourdieu's contention was that different social classes embraced different cultural tastes. Such tastes were culturally reproduced and reinforced by a variety of institutional and economic pressures, 'high culture' tending to be defined by social elites as a means of differentiating themselves and excluding those possessed of less cultural capital, as part of the reproduction of cultural and economic power. This is, of course, a vulgar caricature of Bourdieu's arguments but if nothing else it serves to illustrate a more explicit approach to the role of economic class in the stratification of taste. Such approaches have become diluted in much of the self-indulgent postmodernist tidal wave of sociological analyses of consumption.

One of Bourdieu's areas of interest was, of course, food, and a further purpose served by reference to his work lies in the observation that despite the development of multiple feminist/sociological analyses of gender relations and the growth of 'gender studies' as a field of relatively distinct social scientific enquiry, it is difficult to get past socio-economic class as the principle and primary determinant of many life behaviours, choices and opportunities. This is definitely not to say that gender is unimportant but rather that there are continuing (and positive) creative tensions in class/gender analysis that make it extremely difficult to disentangle the relative effects of each on aspects of the micro-social, including consumption, and especially the consumption of food. In many ways, the force of class as an influence on consumption is still afforded analytic priority over all others, rightly or wrongly, in many discussions of taste and consumption.

This can be seen for example in Mennell's (1985) landmark research but can also be detected in the more recent work by Warde and Martens (2000, p. 126) who noted from their survey research findings that there was little to suggest 'a great deal of difference in taste between men and women, either as regards which restaurants to use or what type of dishes to eat'. This is not the same as saying that class has a greater priority in determining food taste but Warde and Martens' study gives the appearance of being influenced, methodologically, by the assumption that it is. Their work represents a 'sensibilist' empiricism that acts as an antidote to stimulating yet perhaps more fanciful sociological commentary on food and eating. More importantly, it reinforces a question implicit in much literature on food and eating as to whether to talk about gender and taste in food given the comparative state of research ignorance, is in itself sensible?

Women's food tastes

A response to the preceding question is to note that while class and gender values are difficult to disentangle, with some irony the 'domestic food literature' reported earlier has tended to be quite effective at describing, within limits, male tastes, but less effective in outlining those of women. As noted earlier, Charles and Kerr (1988, p. 195) found that women in higher social classes attached less importance to meat as part of meals than women in lower social classes. Among the higher social classes, meals were often egg or cheese based, and included beans and other pulses 'without this being felt as a social deprivation'. Charles and Kerr also note that: 'Spaghetti and other pasta and rice-based meals were more frequent and took the place of the traditional meat and two veg'. Both Douglas (1972) and Mennell et al. (1992) claim that middle-class diet is more varied and has greater range than that of the working class. This is supported by Hornsby-Smith (1984) who notes constancy but significant class variations over time in the UK distribution of household expenditure on meat, fish and eggs; dairy products and fats; fruit and vegetables; cereals and other foods. Higher income groups are more likely to drink coffee than tea, purchase pork in preference to lamb, and spend more on wholemeal bread and fresh fruit and vegetable produce. Tomlinson and Warde's (1993) analysis of UK Family Expenditure Survey data for 1968 and 1988 show that there are persistent class-based trends to purchase particular types of food irrespective of price changes. Further, they suggest that though smaller in size in 1988 than in 1968, the manual working class retain distinctive dietary practices supportive of specific class tastes. At the same time, Wilson (1989), among others, has suggested that women have much greater capacity for dietary change than men. The tension between beliefs about what are good for the family in terms of food consumption are constantly tested against women's perceptions of 'good nutrition' and their personal, preferred, ways of eating.

One issue with all the above is that preferences are not the same as 'taste' or indeed 'choice'. The latter in particular remains a problematic concept in that 'choice' implies a state of freedom in consumption that is rarely attainable (see Wood, 2000a). Preferences, like choices, are constrained by economic, social and cultural factors. I may wish to express a preference for eating caviar with my meal tonight but my available income to spend on that meal permits of only a can of sardines. Even my preference, however, is not necessarily linked in any direct way to my taste. I might *prefer* caviar because of its elite social connotations, but I might not *like* it. Anyone who has attended a meal, whether in a domestic residence or restaurant has faced the dilemma of having to eat or not to eat items on the menu for which they have no 'taste'. Such a view of course resonates with that of Finkelstein (1989) who portrays dining out as a mannered act in which participants conform to the edicts and social conventions of the restaurant in an unthinking way. In other words, they behave as they think they should rather than as they wish.

This rather simplistic vignette aside, to talk of class, gendered or other differentiated tastes is to a great extent to put the sociological cart before the philosophical horse. Sociologists of consumption in general, and of food in particular, have yet to address the wider social scientific and humanities literature on taste in a meaningful way (but see Gronow, 1997). Even the strongest and most sustained analysis to date of food taste, Mennell's (1985) magisterial work on the evolution of food taste in France and England, arguably fails to persuade because its analysis relies on Elias' concepts of figurationalism and figurational change, concepts which never seem to be followed through in a consistent way to a clear conclusion. In social research, as in life, definitions are not to be agonized over at the expense of genuine advances in knowledge. Yet responsibility cannot be avoided for making some explicit inroads into definitional questions. The alternative is, as at present in the sociology of food consumption, to abandon such responsibilities in favour of a disconnected multi-inferential melange.

To summarize thus far, we know relatively little about food tastes and preferences in general, let alone how these are differentiated by gender. There is no shortage of hospitality industry mythologies about women's food preferences or indeed general dining behaviour. Women are generally believed to prefer:

- lighter foods, especially lighter meats such as chicken and pork in preference to beef, lamb or game;

- smaller portions than men because they are likely to be more health and/or diet or body conscious;

- fewer courses at any meal, tending to eschew desserts.

Various surveys of customer food selection and dining experience in restaurants have largely failed to differentiate differences according to gender. Even other, better documented aspects of female dining behaviours are also slightly suspect. For example, Mars and Nicod (1984) in their now classic study of waiters found that men were perceived by waiting staff to be better tippers than women because they were more experienced diners (as opposed to, because women have less economic power). Slightly harder evidence comes from Golding (1998, p. 18) who reports a survey where lone businesswomen claimed to frequently 'experience leering waiters and patronising managers with more than 70 per cent feeling that service

Hospitality, Leisure & Tourism Series

was "secondary" purely because of their gender'. Also when dining with a male, 74 per cent of those women surveyed said that waiters assumed the man to be settling the bill and selecting the wine, while 41 per cent claimed to feel uncomfortable dining alone and 62 per cent chose to eat in their rooms.

Women dining out – some contextual considerations

If, in the absence of extensive hard evidence on women's food tastes, we are looking for Mertonian-like middle range explanations of how such tastes might be identified and analysed, then existing social contexts of analysis provide the only real clue to taste and preference formation. Of undoubted importance in the eating out context in this regard is the concept of the meal experience promulgated by Campbell-Smith (1967) which is to be found, explicitly and implicitly, as a reference point in most major commentaries on dining out as a social phenomenon. The concept of the meal experience as defined by Campbell-Smith posits that customer satisfaction in dining out can be attributed to multiple environmental factors and not simply food choice and food quality. This view has long dominated marketing theory and practice in the hospitality industry despite, in the last 10 years, becoming increasingly suspect as research evidence accumulates suggesting that available food choice, price and quality are exactly what consumers prioritize when dining out (see Wood, 2000b for a review).

Finkelstein's (1989, p. 3) provocative sociological analysis of dining out begins from the point of view that restaurants offer a 'meal experience'. According to Finkelstein, contemporary dining out has much to do with self-presentation and 'the mediation of social relations through images of what is currently valued, accepted and fashionable'. Culturally, restaurants are regarded as places where excitement, pleasure and a sense of well-being will be experienced and these and other images such as wealth and luxury, are represented iconically within restaurants through such means as ambience, décor, furnishings, lighting and tableware. So important are these iconic representations of people's emotional expectations, Finkelstein (1989, p. 3) argues, that the 'physical appearance of the restaurant, its ambience and décor, are as important to the event of dining out as are the comestibles'. Individuals believe themselves to be acting from choice when they dine out and they have expectations that restaurants will help them realize certain desires. These are not simply 'objective' desires – for good food and service – but expectations that restaurants will satisfy deeper emotional desires for status and belongingness. The fact that restaurants in all their varieties claim to be able to offer such satisfaction and indeed embody these desires is, however, indicative of how emotions are transformed into commodities and 'sold' back to individuals as if they were consumer items.

Finkelstein's analysis has attracted its supporters (see Wood, 1995) but also its detractors. Warde and Martens (2000) take issue with Finkelstein, the evidence derived from their study claiming to show that restaurant diners not only exercise control over the dining context but profess and demonstrate multiple forms of independent enjoyment when dining out. In short, both Finkelstein and Warde and Martens adopt an approach based on the idea that motivations for dining out centre on some concept of a 'meal experience'. However, a close reading of both Finkelstein and Warde and Martens does raise the question of whether the position developed in each study is of sufficient methodological sophistication and rigour to support a genuine contrast or conflict of empirical evidence.

Warde and Martens' position is to some degree reached by the rejection of claims made, *inter alia*, by Wood (1995) that domestic and public dining have increasingly converged. This convergence takes the form of public menus coming to increasingly represent the structured dining of the home, with greater similarity between home and external menus and a concomitant overall reduction in the choices available to consumers (see also Wood, 2000b). This 'interpenetration' of private and public dining is supported by advances in technology which support the illusion of choice but have increasingly allowed foods previously available almost exclusively in the public domain to be purchased at the supermarket and consumed at home. Warde and Martens (2000) are unhappy with this view, instead agreeing with Mennell (1985) that increasing variety is a feature of both public and private dining. They claim that writers on convergence have exaggerated trends in convergence and the reduction of choice.

Hospitality, Leisure & Tourism Series

The rejection of convergence views of dining is a necessary condition for any theoretical and empirical position that valourizes bourgeois notions of human choice, preference and individual (or individually derived) models of taste. Indeed, the whole edifice of market segmentation and product differentiation is not only critical to academic marketing theory but to the very maintenance of capitalist–bourgeois notions of individuality and difference. Warde and Martens are quite correct to remind us that trends in both theorizing and the identification and analysis of data can easily be derailed and diverted. These authors, however, are uncomfortably short of persuasive evidence to support their tentative rejection of the convergence thesis (actually multiple convergence theses in the sociology of consumption). This need not matter if an emphasis on convergence can be shown, in the context of food and eating, to be theoretically and empirically partial, incomplete or plain wrong. The problem is, this has not (yet) been the case.

A perhaps more important limitation of all the literature on dining out is the tendency to treat the concept of the 'meal experience' as a hermetically sealed black box with inputs and outputs but no discernible insight into the workings of the box itself. Campbell-Smith (1967) provides the inputs, and is echoed by Finkelstein among others. These two authors are, however, concerned with two very different types of input. For Campbell-Smith, inputs into the meal experience are interior to the restaurant, that is, generated by the restaurant itself, presumably through the interpretation of the external world by the restaurant operator. For Finkelstein, as might be expected, inputs come in the form of the extent to which the restaurant is firmly located within society and societal influences permeate and shape the restaurant. In their study, Warde and Martens tend to concentrate on what they construe to be positive outputs of control and enjoyment, or the consumer's experiential record of the meal experience, a trend present in other studies as well (see Wood, 2000b for a short summary).

If there is a missing link in the dining out literature it is between production and consumption. In respect of gender, as the earlier discussion of sociologies of domestic dining demonstrated, there is a clear relationship between the gendered division of labour and food consumption. Comparable analyses for public dining exists in fragmented strands in human resource management studies of the hospitality industry (see Wood, 1997) but have not yet been fully worked through in the context of the sociology of food and eating. Consumption-oriented studies arguably underplay production–consumption relationships even where they articulate different arguments about the experiential aspects of dining out, as is the case with Warde and Martens (2000), and Finkelstein (1989). In contrast, one of the strengths of convergence views of choice, taste and selection in human behaviour is the way in which links are maintained between production *and* consumption. This is noticeable, for example, in recent debates about McDonaldization (Ritzer, 2000). However flawed the concept of McDonaldization may be (see Wood, 1998) it offers a holistic view of dining relationships which is absent from consumption-oriented studies like those by Warde and Martens, and Finkelstein.

In general however, it must be conceded that attempts at holistic analysis of food systems, embracing systematic investigation of production–consumption relations have themselves not been noticeably successful. The term 'food system' is commonly construed to mean the totality of production, processing, distribution, retailing, consumption and disposal of food. No wonder, then, that analysis pitched at this grand level has been limited in investigative utility. The problem of scale is, not, however, the only difficulty, as Beardsworth and Kiel remind us:

> The use of the term 'food system' may conjure up an idea of a formally organized set of links between food production, distribution and consumption which is arranged according to some well-thought-out plan or scheme... such a model is inappropriate and unworkable. However, if we are careful not to assume that there is some underlying plan which informs its organization, the term food system can be a convenient way of drawing attention to the particular character of the complex of interdependent interrelationships associated with the production and distribution of food... (Beardsworth and Kiel, 1997, pp. 32–32)

In short, food systems are not normally mechanistically intentioned: serendipity can play a role in both the form and action of a system. Beardsworth and Kiel (1997) add to this the observation that in discussing systems, there is a tendency to prefer simplistic conceptions of stasis, that is, systems are depicted at a moment in time, with little regard for how they change over time. Temporality is of course at the heart of the 'diminishing contrasts, increasing varieties' argument of Mennell (1985) and there is a temptation to assert that any understanding of gendered food tastes can only realistically be achieved if we engage in longitudinal analysis, hardly a practical proposition.

From context to actuality

If longitudinal analysis has its problems, then holistic approaches to the production–consumption relationship based on a macro-systems approach are not the only analytic alternatives available to us. More pragmatic models that sustain a focus on the relationship between production and consumption are possible. In the context of gendered food tastes, and women's food tastes in particular, this may in the short term add little in the way of new knowledge but it does provide a model for future investigation. Arguably, more such models are needed as investigative tools in the sociology of food and eating, the development of which over the last 25 years has been characterized in both empirical and theoretical terms by piecemeal empirical contributions and largely partial theoretical syntheses.

To pursue this strategy is to some focus on a number of questions designed to establish comparisons between production and consumption in the private and public domains. The former we have already explored in terms of women's domestic roles as purchasers and preparers of food. We have seen that the evidence points to these roles being influenced by economic and class concerns but that in general there is a *prima facie* case that notwithstanding these influences, women are in terms of equality disadvantaged in their relationships to these roles vis-à-vis men. What is less clear is whether women's roles in this respect create differences in taste. In the public domain it is necessary to acknowledge that a number of facets of the production–consumption relationship differ. In general, men are public cooks (chefs) while women tend to dominate the 'server' category as waiting staff, but often in marginal, poorly paid part time jobs. The hospitality industry has one of the highest proportions of women managers of any, yet most are concentrated not in positions of senior operational responsibility but in functional roles such as human resource and marketing management.

On the consumption side of the equation, the 'domestic literature' tells us that the production role is a complex one for women, often involving denial of their own pleasures and/or tastes in terms of the choice and selection of foods as they cater for their male partners and families. Purchase and preparation of food is experienced as a form of powerlessness, as an onerous duty and responsibility rather than freedom. Social context seems to admit that the performance of these functions involves a 'setting aside' of women's own preferences as one means of reducing the complexity of decision making in the process of provision.

The situation is far less clear in the public domain. Conventional research wisdom suggests that women are less likely to dine out independently than men, with women's presence in restaurants more often than not attributable to them accompanying husbands or male partners or as part of a family unit. Women's (lower) discretionary spending power has also been identified as a factor in their reduced incidence of public dining. Golding's (1998) comments noted earlier suggest that it is harder for women to dine in public and that they are treated less favourably than men, a point which links closely to the control of 'space' for women in public hospitality settings. In her seminal paper on this topic, Carmouche (1983) indicates how the history of British hospitality charts the 'separation' of women in public hospitality organizations, not least in the public houses where women have in the past been both explicitly and implicitly excluded from the public bar and 'confined' to the lounge.

Of course, much has changed in the UK in the last 20 years, although the position in other countries is less clear. Despite this, there is remarkably little that the locational context of dining tells us about gendered taste. The context of provision is another matter. The 'domestic literature' yields the important

Hospitality, Leisure & Tourism Series

observation that menus are planned around male tastes, with an emphasis on 'heavy' foods that are 'typically male'. Any inspection of restaurant menus, even allowing for variations in local and national taste, reveals similar forces at work. Although women have made inroads into the world of professional cookery, it is still dominated by men. A menu is, by definition, a statement of what a restaurant is prepared to offer – the customer's possible range of choice is predetermined. Independent restaurateurs appear to adopt and change their menus only slowly and then by reference to local competition rather than wider social influences (Auty, 1992). The menu is, in the broadest sense, a male artefact. Even where it makes provision for gendered differences in food taste, such provision is a male conceptualization of such taste or perspective on it.

Such a view invites an almost instinctive negative response, an 'harrumphing' of risible disbelief. How might it be, the question could be posed, given the plurality of food styles, cuisines and individual tastes, that such a distorted view of restaurant food provision can be sustained? The point is, of course, that the plurality of food styles and cuisines in a world characterized by global agribusiness, strong global and regional food chains and a growing gap between rich and poor is a lot less plural than at first appears, as indeed is the supposed plurality of food tastes which are conditioned by the very cultural influences that have become embattled by these forces. As Roland Barthes (1973) noted, taste in food and eating, including public dining culture, is a matter of national and other identity. By definition, a national identity mediated through food must constitute a framework of permissible tastes that draws in the majority of people. When Warde and Martens (2000) find that there is apparently little difference between men and women's tastes in food selection when dining out it is an indicator not of increased variety or pluralism but of increased homogeneity, an irony that escapes them. Those who argue a 'more choice' or 'some choice' position in relation to food consumption are guilty of promulgating a liberal delusion in a world where the manifest trend is towards 'little choice' or 'no choice'. We may have to contend with the possibility that gendered differences in taste (if they exist at all) might disappear as a result of levelling. One thing seems certain, if gendered differences in taste exist, there is no reason to suppose they are any less amenable to analysis in terms of patriarchal relations than any other social phenomenon. Unless, however, a stronger and more coherent research agenda can be developed to replace the existing patchwork of theoretical speculation and occasional empirical insight, we may have to reconcile ourselves to the possibility that we will never know.

Bibliography

Auty, S. (1992). Consumer choice and segmentation in the restaurant industry. *The Service Industries Journal* **12** (3), pp. 324–339.

Barthes, R. (1973). *Mythologies*. London: Paladin.

Beardsworth, A. and Kiel, T. (1997). *Sociology on the Menu: An Invitation to the Study of Food and Society*. London: Routledge.

Bourdieu, P. (1984). *Distinction: A Social Critique of the Judgement of Taste*. London: Routledge and Kegan Paul.

Campbell-Smith, G. (1967). *The Marketing of the Meal Experience*. London: Surrey University Press.

Carmouche, R. (1983). Gender and social consumption. *The Service Industries Journal* **3** (1), 49–62.

Charles, N. and Kerr, M. (1988). *Women, Food and Families*. Manchester: Manchester University Press.

Coxon, T. (1983). Men in the kitchen: notes from a cookery class. In *The Sociology of Food and Eating* (A. Murcott, Ed.). Farnborough: Gower, pp. 172–177.

Dare, S. (1988). Too many cooks? Food acceptability and women's work in the informal economy. In *Food Acceptability* (D. Thomson, Ed.). London: Elsevier, pp. 143–153.

Douglas, M. (1972). Deciphering a meal. In *Implicit Meanings* (M. Douglas, Ed.). London: Routledge and Kegan Paul, pp. 249–175.

Ellis, R. (1983) The way to a man's heart: food in the violent home. In *The Sociology of Food and Eating* (A. Murcott, Ed.). Farnborough: Gower, pp. 164–171.

Erlichman, J. (1993). Holding the pursestrings. *The Guardian*, 21 December, p. 6.

Finkelstein, J. (1989). *Dining Out: A Sociology of Modern Manners*. Cambridge: Polity Press.

Hospitality, Leisure & Tourism Series

Golding, C. (1998). Hotels must update attitudes to women. *Caterer and Hotelkeeper*, 10 September, p. 18.

Gronow, J. (1997). *The Sociology of Taste*. London: Routledge.

Hornsby-Smith, M.P. (1984). Sociological aspects of food behaviour: an analysis of recent trends in Britain. *Journal of Consumer Studies and Home Economics* **8**, 199–216.

Jerome, N.W., Kandel, J. and Pelto, G. (Eds) (1980). *Nutritional Anthropology*. Pleasantville: Redgrave Publishing.

Kerr, M. and Charles, N. (1986). Servers and providers: the distribution of food within the family. *Sociology* **34**, 115–157.

Mars, G. and Nicod, M. (1984). *The World of Waiters*. London: George Allen and Unwin.

Mennell, S. (1985). *All Manners of Food: Eating and Taste in England and France from the Middle Ages to the Present*. Oxford: Basil Blackwell.

Mennell, S., Murcott, A. and van Otterloo, A. (1992). *The Sociology of Food: Eating, Diet and Culture*. London: Sage Publications.

Murcott, A. (1982). On the social significance of the 'cooked dinner' in South Wales. *Social Science Information* **21**, 677–696.

Ritzer, G. (2000). *The McDonaldization of Society*. London: Pine Forge Press.

Rosenberg, E.M. (1980). Sex differential nutrition. In *Nutritional Anthropology* (N.W. Jerome, J. Kandel and G. Pelto, Eds). Pleasantville: Redgrave Publishing, pp. 181–204.

Simoons, F.J. (1967). *Eat Not this Flesh*. Madison: University of Wisconsin Press.

Tomlinson, M. and Warde, A. (1993). Social class and change in eating habits. *British Food Journal* **95**, 3–10.

Warde, A. and Martens, L. (2000). *Eating Out: Social Differentiation, Consumption and Pleasure*. Cambridge: Cambridge University Press.

Wilson, G. (1989). Family food systems: preventive health and dietary change: a policy to increase the health divide. *Journal of Social Policy* **18**, 167–185.

Wood, R.C. (1995). *The Sociology of the Meal*. Edinburgh: Edinburgh University Press.

Wood, R.C. (1997). *Working in Hotels and Catering*. London: Thomson Learning.

Wood, R.C. (1998). New wine in old bottles: critical limitations of the McDonaldization thesis – the case of hospitality services. In *McDonaldization Revisited: Critical Essays on Consumer Culture* (M. Alfino et al., Eds). Wetsport: Praeger, pp. 85–104.

Wood, R.C. (2000). Is food an art form? Pretentiousness and pomposity in cookery. In *Strategic Questions in Food and Beverage Management* (R.C. Wood, Ed.). Oxford: Butterworth-Heinemann, pp. 153–171.

Wood, R.C. (2000a). What do we really know about the requirements of food and beverage consumers? Food and beverage markets in the modern age. In *Strategic Questions in Food and Beverage Management* (R.C. Wood, Ed.). Oxford: Butterworth-Heinemann, pp. 10–27.

Wood, R.C. (2000b). How important is the meal experience? Choices, menus and dining environments. In *Strategic Questions in Food and Beverage Management* (R.C. Wood, Ed.). Oxford: Butterworth-Heinemann, pp. 28–47.

CHAPTER 9

Developing a taste for health

David Fouillé

Introduction

In the current context of food crisis, emphasis on the sociology of food is increasing in search for a rationalization of modern food consumption patterns (Poulain, 2002). Whereas food availability has long been of widespread concern, especially in underdeveloped countries, the nature of food consumption within developed countries is now climbing up the political agenda.

The recent growth in levels of consumption of convenience foods, within both domestic and commercial settings, is well documented. However, recent high profile food scandals have raised questions regarding not only the amount of food consumed, but also the general condition of that food and the consequences of consumption for our health.

In this chapter food consumption will be analysed in the light of growing health awareness. Attention will be given to the changing status of food, not so much in terms of the expression of identity, but rather regarding the intrinsic value of food. Finally, the dimension of taste will be considered in relation to health and global environmental concerns.

Health awareness

Health and lifestyles

Although more evident, food-related health concerns are not new. In ancient Greece, Hippocrates' medicine was based on four categories of food and their relationship to four emotional conditions: wet, dry, hot and cold. *Diaita* (lifestyle in Greek) was associated with nutrition, and the Greek scholars ordered that certain types of food be avoided, possibly to prevent noisy and odoriferous intrusions in the philosophical debates (Skrabanek, 1994). Personal health concerns were associated with virtuous values, and Skrabanek further relates how healthy eating was endorsed by certain movements in the belief that illness and premature death could be avoided by means of a discriminating lifestyle: less meat, less fats, less sugar, less alcohol, and less sex.

Such concerns and restrictions have been maintained throughout the centuries, most obviously through religious dictates regarding food preparation and consumption. Meat in particular has always been and still remains a controversial food item, either due to its inherent ambivalent connotations of life and death (Poulain, 2002), or through the more straightforward belief that meat contains toxic blood and germs (Skrabanek, 1994).

It is interesting to note that in the majority of developed nations dining out has grown in popularity in recent years (refer to Chapter 5), yet despite this apparent acceptance of dining out as a key leisure activity, we have seen the emergence of a media obsession with health concerns about the nature of our diet (Fischler, 1993).

Food has shifted from being a potentially unconsciously accepted part of everyday life to a source of greater attention, particularly in relation to health. The attention surrounding what we eat is largely related to our dual concerns for health and pleasure, and Fischler (1993) examines this pattern in various human societies: is pleasure trustworthy and guided by the wisdom of our bodies, or is it on the contrary a misleading and hazardous attraction? The general consensus seems to be that superior health stems from restriction and discernment within our food consumption patterns (Gronow, 1997).

Despite growing health concerns in populations in the last 30 years in particular, there seems to be a persisting confusion about the meaning of 'healthy'. The perception of 'healthy' according to working class standards, as identified by Bourdieu (in Wood, 1995) certainly differs from the bourgeois standards that emerged since the 1970s. Where meals of the working class are focused on compensating for the energy expenditure from long hours of heavy work, the bourgeois display greater concern for health and physical appearance through personal asceticism (Bisogni et al., 2002; Gronow, 1997).

Responsibility of the food industry

It has been suggested that the perceived spread of food-related diseases and the promotion of unhealthy eating are largely endorsed by a global food industry. It is believed by some that responsibility for a pattern of unhealthy food production, with livestock being fed hormones and antibiotics, waters being infected by animal slurry (Ford, 2000), and genetically modified organisms lying latent, rests with multinational food companies. The potentially contradictory motives of profit generation and concern for the health of consumers are often highlighted, as are some of the marketing techniques of certain companies. Such techniques may encourage the adoption of unbalanced diets, the consequences of which are particularly concerning in countries in which energy expense from physical activities is in decline (Hoffman, 2001). There is particular concern that aggressive marketing campaigns aimed at children might result in the adoption of diets which fall short of meeting basic nutritional requirements. American children, for instance, achieve 50 per cent of their energy intake through added fat and sugar in snacks and soft drinks (Nestle, 2000), a pattern which is likely to be spreading under the influence of market globalization. There is also an evident trend among food manufacturers to enhance food value by claims related to health. Certain dubious advertising practices emphasize the properties of certain foods that apparently lower cholesterol or reduce the risk of contracting cancer, all 'as part of a healthy diet' (Nestle, 2000). Such claims may encourage misconceptions among consumers.

Hoffman (2001) claims that dietary problems are related to changing lifestyles, and the phenomenon of urbanization in particular. Not only are urban populations less active, they are also much more reliant on convenience and prepared foods, whether within the home or in restaurants.

Within this context the obvious challenge is how to encourage widespread uptake of healthier food choices.

What we eat, and how we eat it

As noted in chapters throughout this text, food consumption has long been associated with the display of one's identity. It is emphasized by the specificity of humans to be omnivorous, which is synonymous with choice, autonomy and adaptability (Fischler, 1993). However, Fischler further outlines that this autonomy is also bound by the constraint of variety. Variety is the source of nutritious elements (proteins, vitamins, minerals, etc.) humans rely on in their complex nutritional system. This paradox touched upon by Fischler relates to the ambiguous neophobia and neophilia of humans towards food, characterized by a need to explore new foods to acquire vital nutriments, and a vital necessity to beware of potential dangers from food. This paradox in modern developed societies is further complicated by our realization that foods which have long been considered safe and even health promoting, can in fact be a source of danger. Many of our most familiar foods are now surrounded with distrust and hesitation. Poulain (2002) highlights how this has led, to an extent, to commercial food consumption moving from being associated purely with positive gastronomic and leisure interests to one underpinned by serious social and scientific considerations, often driven by those in the academic community.

Obesity is an increasingly common food-related disorder and it is possibly the most obvious indication of the radical changes in food consumption patterns that have occurred since the beginning of the twentieth century. The main observation is a revolution of food-related diseases. Whereas food deficiencies were the major cause of food-related death and illness worldwide at the turn of the nineteenth century, many chronic conditions of the twenty-first century, such as coronary heart disease, diabetes, stroke or high blood pressure, are related to food excess (Nestle, 2000). It seems that this problem has been exacerbated by the relentless growth in the consumption of foods in US-style fast-food restaurants and of pre-prepared convenience foods at home (Ford, 2000; Miller, 1996). If one accepts the concept of McDonaldization (Ritzer, 2000) as the inevitable model for the evolution of many economic and social systems and the reported likely consequences of globalization, then this trend may well continue. Nestle (2000) observes how American children (but the pattern can be observed in most western societies, and is growing in developing countries) are literally bombarded with commercials promoting fast-food, snack foods and soft drinks, the consequences of which will be examined later. In such circumstances, food becomes a commodity like any other, the consumption of which receives little consideration.

Counter trends

Consequences of food insecurity

Despite such a pessimistic outlook, there is evidence to suggest that food-related health concerns are now more prevalent, albeit as a consequence of food scandals of the past two decades, which were largely uncovered by the media. In 1996 an announcement was made in Great Britain of a potential link between bovine spongiform encephalopathy (BSE) and the human Creutzfeld-Jakob disease. This not only resulted in a dramatic decline in beef consumption (and meat consumption in general) across Europe (Regmi and Gehlhar, 2001), but it also revealed somewhat perverted, yet widespread, food production practices: vegetarian cows fed meat-based food, and even worse, cows being fed beef. The consequent headlines such as 'Cannibal cows' and 'Frankenfood' raised serious health concerns among consumers, and distrust about the quality of many foods.

By encouraging people to choose a more healthy way of eating, there is also an invitation to a more personal eating, and hence a discovery (and even re-discovery) of certain foodstuffs. The current trend is indeed to move away from mass consumption, and hence to look for new foods. Although this is not an unusual inclination for the omnivorous human, the search for new foods in human history is rather related to seasonality, changing ecosystems or socio-economic evolution (Fischler, 1993). This pattern might indeed look like an anachronism in a global world where food is not scarce any more (at least among most developed countries), it is however a genuine one. The US Departments of Agriculture and Health and Human Services, for instance, advise that five to nine portions of fruit and vegetables should be eaten every day (Regmi and Gehlhar, 2001). If such patterns are to be followed, there is a need for a more attractive offer in order to avoid strong reluctance due to taste monotony. Hence the search for new foodstuffs.

Food remains an essential element of daily life, not just for matters of pleasure or consumption, but for the purpose of maintaining life. As such, food is thought to remain a major source of pleasure in an activity that, in human cultures, occupies very little time every day (Friedlander et al., 1999). That time, however, is expected to be highly qualitative in a busy daily schedule where lunch and dinner could often be the only relaxed moments. Thus, growing health awareness and an emerging self-consciousness seem to lead to a pursuit of better quality food, and indeed tastier food. The act of eating is highly affective (Friedlander et al., 1999), an intimate activity hardly shared with others, although eating remains a highly social activity. Fischler (1993) elevates the incorporation of food to a climax, the unique act of integrating the external world into the internal body. The quest in modern developed societies therefore is not just to eat for survival, but also to eat for one's pleasure and satisfaction beyond the mere physiological value of the food consumed. The strongly growing environmental awareness of the past three decades has contributed to that quest (Goldstein, 2001), and links two motives of self-satisfaction: the satisfaction to contribute to a healthier environment, and the belief to eat healthier.

Questing quality

Consumer anxiety has stimulated interest in alternative food products which have less associated risk. The dramatic increase in recent years in demand for organic produce (most evident to date in the retail rather that the restaurant sector) reflects this desire to minimize risk. Miller (1996) notes an increased awareness among consumers about the nature of food production and distribution and about the consequences of consumption. It seems that the demand for organic foods reflects a range of emerging concerns including the environmental impact of food production, the need to stimulate local economies, the traceability of produce, and a belief that money spent on organic brings health maintenance and tastier foods (Goldstein, 2001). Ford (2000) is encouraged by his identification of a gradual change in the way in which consumers are being encouraged to adapt their food preferences. He sees a move away from delivering frightening messages on the need for personal constraint, to a more positive emphasis on the connection between food choice and personal well-being.

The move from constraint to choice appears as a prerequisite to a genuinely healthier lifestyle. This optimistic approach to the achievement of health through appropriate diets challenges the dominant belief that all that is tasty and attractive is necessarily unhealthy.

The health benefits of eating quality food are generally accepted, and the trend is therefore to switch from unhealthy foodstuffs (and hence unhealthy tastes) to a wider variety of foods, in particular fruit and vegetables. Consequently, there is a tendency to shift from processed food to more genuine and plain foods with distinct attributes. The changing status of meat underlines this tendency, given that the avoidance of meat in particular has become a question of choice rather than necessity, and is consumed for its taste rather than its symbolic status (Miele, 1999).

From taste to health

Negative health implications of McDonaldized food habits have been established, particularly for children, who are far from meeting dietary recommendations. Considering the issues of mass culture, Warde (1997) identifies the ubiquity of McDonald's and Coca-Cola as contributing to a loss of taste diversity. There is indeed a widespread promotion of fried foods, salt and sugar, which is particularly prejudicial to children, who already have an established neophobia towards food, and a general preference for the accessible tastes of sugar and salt. Taste is established at an early age, and deviant patterns of taste (or indeed standardized patterns of taste), such as those imposed by fast and junk food diets, will therefore be extremely difficult to alter at a later stage.

As far back as 1825, Brillat-Savarin (1982) highlighted the relationship between health and taste, suggesting that by means of taste (and smell, both being closely associated), comestible food can generally be distinguished from non-comestible or rotten food. However, by modern processing and flavouring of food, the health factor, or indeed unhealthy constitution, is concealed. Therefore, even though modern technology should protect us from food hazards, it also facilitates the production of foods which are inherently unhealthy.

A restrictive approach to food, nourished by well established beliefs and customs, remains a common approach in efforts to maintain health. However, there is also a growing awareness and acceptance of a relationship between food and pleasure (Ford, 2000). Whereas food abundance and abuse is commonly accepted as being unhealthy, restrictions in terms of quantity are being compensated by an improved quality of what we eat. Food taste and quality are re-emerging as the very source of palatable pleasure. The current growing health awareness seems therefore to largely involve, directly or somewhat indirectly, the dimension of taste. Healthy food is related to food variety (Nestle, 2000; Regmi and Gehlahr, 2001), and even more, to enjoyment (Ford, 2000). Rising food fears, and the subsequent growing consciousness of what arrives on our plates, might have had an unexpected and positive impact on the ethics of food production, on health and on taste.

Better taste for better health

Educating taste

Beyond health, taste is generally the main criteria for food choice, likes and dislikes driving preferences (Friedlander, 1999). The origin of taste (in terms of likes and dislikes) remains ambiguous, but certainly relies on both innate and socially acquired factors (Fischler, 1993; Rigal, 2002). Dominant patterns have been observed, both in children and adults: a preference for sweet taste rather than bitter taste, and an equal attraction (neophilia) and distrust (neophobia) towards new foods (Friedlander et al., 1999; Rigal, 2002). Such patterns, however, are more acute with children, and the process of overcoming these tendencies relies on sensorial education (Rigal, 2002). Rigal identifies that it is a simpler process to influence children's food tastes during their formative years, rather than to challenge personal tastes that have developed over time. Early familiarity with a wide variety of foods encourages children to be more accepting of new foods later in life (Fischler, 1993). Practical examples of this form of taste education can be identified, such as in France where most young children take their lunch in school canteens, and where much emphasis is placed on the provision of varied, well-balanced meals.

The importance of developing a contact with foodstuffs is further supported by Rigal (2002), who claims that a more positive approach to food is the key to the acceptance of greater varieties of foods. Her main claim is to move away from a mere classification of foods into likes, dislikes, healthy or unhealthy, and to accurately introduce children to what they eat. Cognitive taste, Rigal further argues, grows with every individual, and thus influences the food choices of adults. Early education of taste could then break the barriers of food monotony developed in prosaic (in terms of taste) societies, and contribute to greater health awareness through a better understanding of food. The effect of health awareness among children should not be underestimated, and must be considered at an early stage, when education is still shaping their minds and taste. This of course is only possible if children are educated in health and taste by their parents, who need to be educated themselves. Unfortunately, as Ford (2000) observes, modern meals are rarely taken together, and the family occupation of preparing a meal is disappearing altogether, sacrificed to a time-stressed modern world. Fischler (1993) identifies how the loss of inter-generation food customs transmission is also lethal to taste.

The organic revelation

Food has undergone some radical changes within two centuries. Whereas in 1825 Brillat-Savarin advocated a lavish way of eating, the late nineteenth century was marked by strong ascetic beliefs (Skrabanek, 1994). The early to mid-twentieth century was of course marked by restrictions due to two world wars. The 1980s and 1990s in turn witnessed the emergence of a more abundant eating routine, to the extent that food became omnipresent in our lives. Daily food contacts increased greatly in the past two decades in the form of snacks and junk food in particular (Poulain, 2002). However, both moralization and liberalization of food appear excessive. Moreover, they seem to largely neglect the dimensions of quality and taste.

If food expenses are growing worldwide, the emphasis seems to rather be on food attributes relative to quality and taste. Organic food in particular is increasingly in demand, with growth rates of 15–30 per cent in Europe, the United States and Japan for 5 years (Regmi and Gehlhar, 2001). The organic food revolution not only stands for better health through less pesticides and artificial fertilizers, it essentially stands for a greater transparency and understanding of food production (Goldstein, 2001).

Miller (1996) identifies how organic food consumers are largely influenced by food safety issues in particular. As they seek a better balanced diet, they are also concerned about the amount of chemicals, hormones and pollution they consume. The fact that organic is perceived to taste better, however remote it might seem from primary concerns, is a crucial factor influencing more recent consumption patterns. There seems to be a (re)-discovery of certain foods and tastes in regard to fruit and vegetables in particular, as consumers spot varieties they had either forgotten about, or largely ignored. Furthermore, consumers seem to place greater emphasis on the intrinsic attributes of their food, which has to taste and look better (Miller, 1996). Hence, consumers see a connection between their health and the wider benefits of what they eat: taste and pleasure (Ford, 2000; Miller, 1996).

Organic food brings consumers closer to their food and to food production methods (Goldstein, 2001). There is a shift away from mass consumption, and an appeal for more transparent production and more educated eating, as opposed to the fat-free explosion identified by Miller (1996), stimulated by a misunderstood (and most probably voluntarily misleading) message engendered by the profit motive. Organic, Miller further underlines, needs a greater commitment from consumers, and is therefore likely to hold longer and stronger.

Globalizing taste

The main changes in diet identified by Ford (2000), mainly a shift from the obsession with loosing weight to the enjoyment of healthy food, is also sustained by globalization in various ways. First, a food crisis is frequently the cause of an identity crisis, and leads consumers to look at new food varieties and preparations (Poulain, 2002). Thus, the potential health benefits of particular and unusual foodstuffs and diets have contributed to the integration of new tastes in traditional national cooking. The integration in western, developed countries of a range of new tastes from Asia in particular, facilitated by a more accessible world, is very representative of this pattern, and nuoc mam, various sambals, nasi goreng, sushi or curry are now well established in western cuisine (Ford, 2000). Many modern restaurants, following the trend, offer some form of fusion food, where lemon grass and coriander, for instance, add to the taste of familiar dishes.

Further, Poulain (2002) identifies a three-fold dimension of globalization: the disappearing of certain food singularities, the emergence of new, mingled food forms, and the cross-cultural diffusion of certain culinary products and practices. Whereas the first contributes to a loss of certain food identities and hence tastes, the latter two undoubtedly add new tastes to existing ones, and increase the taste range available to particular cultures. However, Poulain further identifies how culture also constrains the integration of particular food identities. The success of a guest cuisine is largely dependent on adapting to the host culture, which is largely the case with most of the ethnic restaurants evident in Western societies (Ford, 2000; Poulain, 2002). New tastes, however authentic, are nevertheless available.

Finally, although many socio-cultural identities seem to merge within the process of globalization, globalization has in fact generated a large number of social and political movements, some of which are passionately concerned with food production and consumption (Miele, 1999). The aspiration of these movements is that food be carefully considered as a vital element,

Hospitality, Leisure & Tourism Series

and that food production methods be in harmony with consumption needs and respectful of the environment. Beyond the strong ethical engagement of such movements, there is a strong contribution to the wider emergence of better food, largely supporting the organic growth (Bisogni et al., 2002). Further, food identities are claimed back, and 'traditional' and 'authentic' food stuffs regain high ethical and moral value (Miele, 1999). Poulain (2002) also identifies this pattern in the way France has largely (re)-developed regional cuisine and patrimonial gastronomy since the 1980s, as a response to the homogenization of alimentary taste. In times of social instability and political insecurity, seeking the comfort of tasty food appears like a healthy reaction.

Conclusion

Growing health concerns are rational reactions to various food issues that have emerged in the past few decades. The fact that many modern conditions such as obesity, cardio-vascular disorders and even certain forms of cancer are linked to food consumption is a growing concern in both developed and developing countries (Hoffman, 2001).

However, particular attention is growing around two dimensions of better food: one relative to health, with an emphasis on improved food production systems, one relative to taste, and recollecting that food, beyond its vital value, has a physiological and emotional dimension.

Bibliography

Bisogni, C., Connors, M., Devine, C. and Sobal, J. (2002). Who we are and how we eat: a qualitative study of identities in food choice. *Journal of Nutrition, Education and Behaviour* **34** (3), 128–140.

Brillat-Savarin, J.A. (1982). *Physiologie du Goût*. Paris: Flammarion.

Fischler, C. (1993). *L'homnivore*. Paris: Points.

Ford, B. (2000). The taste of tomorrow: globalization is coming home to dinner. *Futurist* **34** (6), 41–46.

Friedlander, J., Rozin, P. and Sokolov, R. (1999). Everyday life: ordinary pleasures, rituals and taboos. *Social Research* **66** (1), 1–35.

Goldstein, J. (2001). The evolution of the organic food revolution. *Business* **23** (3), 31–33.

Gronow, J. (1997). *The Sociology of Taste*. London: Routledge.

Hoffman, D.J. (2001). Obesity in developing countries: causes and implications. *Food, Nutrition and Agriculture*. FAO Publications.

Miele, M. (1999). Short circuits: new trends in the consumption of food and the changing status of meat. *International Planning Studies* **4** (3), 373–388.

Miller, C. (1996). Challenge to fat-free. *Marketing News* **30** (22), 1–2.

Nestle, M. (2000). Changing the diet of a nation: Population/ regulatory strategies for a developed economy. *Asia Pacific Journal of Clinical Nutrition* **9** (Suppl), 33–40.

Platzman, A. (1998). Eating out fast, but healthfully: is it possible? *Environmental Nutrition* **21** (7), 1–2.

Poulain, J.P. (2002). *Sociologies de L'Alimentation*. Paris: Presses Universitaires de France.

Regmi, A. and Gehlhar, M. (2001). Consumer preferences and concerns shape global food trade. *Food Review* **24** (3), 2–8.

Rigal, N. (2002). La naissance du goût. *Objectif Nutrition* **64**, Juillet, Institut Danone.

Skrabanek, P. (1994). L'alimentation: entre enfer et salut. In *Manger Magique*. Autrement, pp. 169–178.

Warde, A. (1997). *Consumption, Food and Taste: Culinary Antinomies and Commodity Culture*. London: Sage Publications.

Wood, R.C. (1995). *The Sociology of the Meal*. Edinburgh: Edinburgh University Press.

My most memorable meal ever! Hospitality as an emotional experience

Conrad Lashley, Alison Morrison and Sandie Randall

Introduction

The focus of this chapter is on social, as opposed to convenience, eating. This basic distinction is made by Cullen (1994), who suggests that social eating must fulfil certain social functions for it to be successful. The meal experience investigated, therefore, involves more than snacks, 'grazing' activities, 'refuelling', or those with ulterior motives such as business lunches (Lashley, 2000). It engages with the special and memorable occasion, providing insights into aspects concerned with emotions and inherent social dynamics. Meal occasions may be regarded both as an 'object' displaying structure and form as well as an 'event' with physiological, psychological and sociological components (Douglas, 1975), and are recognizable in that they tend to be associated with their cyclical appearance in the household and with social events (Mitchell, 1999). In this respect, Gillespie and Morrison (2001) suggest that consumption holds symbolic emotional value associated with rites of passage, such as graduation, wedding or funeral. Thus, this chapter incorporates sociological perspectives in drawing on the points of view of young consumers of hospitality, and delves into their emotions, associated social practices and value systems. Specifically, it progresses knowledge through an appreciation of the place and composition of a sociable and memorable meal experience within their lives as a structured object that represents a symbolic and emotional event, as supported by Warde and Martens (1998).

The content of the chapter illuminates that hospitality consumed in the home and in commercial settings serves a complex function in that consumption of associated products and services is in part used as a means of making and maintaining social relationships. For as Beardsworth and Keil (1997) emphasize, this adds the dimensions of kinship, friendship and enemyship as integral to the meal experience, as by their nature they cannot be easily divorced from the emotions embodied therein. Furthermore, the behavioural practices associated with the consumption of hospitality exhibit social meaning greater than the activity itself. For as Riley (1994) suggests, the meal reflects something of the social fabric within a country, particularly family, gender, class and age relationships as well as historical traditions. This positions it as a powerful cultural medium, symbolizing relationships and social institutions, and underlies its function in facilitating sociality and reinforcing social order as embodied in the process of repast sharing (Gofton, 1995). Fundamentally the chapter explores guests' emotions underpinning these social dimensions of meal occasions.

Methodology

Data incorporated into this chapter is derived from a pilot study involving 63 first year students registered on a BA in

Hotel and Hospitality Management at a British University. In order to provide a contextual setting, it may be useful to know that the respondents fall into a 17–25 age group, the majority originate from the West of Scotland, with European and overseas students accounting for approximately 15 per cent, and in the main they come from families of average to above-average affluence. They were required to write a 500 words narrative reflecting on their most memorable meal experience, and were guided to structure the content within an analytic framework composed of six dimensions: occasion; company; atmosphere; food; service and setting. Clearly, resultant findings are context, age, life experience, social status and culture dependent. Furthermore, the fact that they are students who have chosen to study hospitality, and that many have work experience in the sector, may mean that the insights are not necessarily atypical of contemporary youth in Britain. While these sampling limitations may detract from generalizability, this is arguably offset by the richness of findings, and the novel and insightful contribution to the existing knowledge base.

Semiotic theory offered a relevant framework for a systematic inquiry that allowed the researchers to interrogate the seemingly everyday language of the narratives for dominant meanings (Saussure, 1974; Barthes, 1973, 1977). Semiotic analysis provides an analytical model that elucidates meaning from texts via a deconstruction of the signifying codes. This can be done in two ways: paradigmatic choices and syntagmatic chains (Saussure, 1974). The former is defined from its distinctiveness and difference of the chosen sign from the other possible choices available; and from the connotations emerging from the choice (Barthes, 1973, 1977). However, the complete meaning of the message results from the selection and combination of these signifiers into syntagmatic chains of meaning. As Storey argues 'the meanings made possible by language are thus the result of the interplay of a network of relationships between combination and selection, similarity and difference' (1993, p. 71). Importantly, Storey emphasizes that the function of such communication is its ability to construct access to a perceived reality, rather than to reflect an 'existing' one.

Thus, in this way respondents' output was 'captured' and the narrative linguistically analysed to provide an indirect portal to their thinking and to surface the structure of their values, feelings and ideas behind their selection of the event, their perceptions and personal evaluations (Gyimothy, 2000). Specifically, analysis took the form of systematic interrogation of every narrative to ascertain its significance via semiotic analysis. The data was categorized in two distinct ways: firstly by asking what is the significance of meaning in what is depicted according to the difference from the alternative choices that were not chosen (paradigmatic); secondly, by looking at the ways the associated choices create comprehensive and complementary chains of similar and dominant meanings (syntagmatic) (Saussure, 1974; Barthes, 1973, 1977). The text was read repeatedly for total immersion. As categories emerged, it became easier to begin to identify the significance of other elements within the narratives as they either confirmed or diverged from the initial themes to initiate further analysis and new classifications. This iterative, constant comparative method (Glaser and Strauss, 1967) underpins the research methodology.

Such a methodology is supported in that it has the potential to reveal respondents' perceived reality of the meal experience, and a deeper dimensionality to the service encounter (Johns and Howard, 1998). This leads Gyimothy (2000) to call for a more holistic and phenomenological approach to analysing consumptions experiences, instead of surveying service journeys according to some rigid, supply-based structure. Thus, narratives can provide a symbolized account of actions, which possess an organizing theme that weaves events into a coherent story of a dedicated consumer activity in which context, or ambience may offer a meaningful experience over and above food (Wood, 1994).

The multi-dimensionality of meals

The following sections explore the broader conceptualizations of the meal experience by investigating the perceptions, symbolized accounts and emotional reactions of respondents to events that they self-selected as representing the most memorable. Discussion is structured within an analytical framework composed of the six dimensions provided to guide the respondents' reflection: nature of the occasion of the meal; fellow diners who made up the company with whom they dined; characteristics that contributed to the atmosphere; food eaten; overall setting and the service provided. Of particular significance is that all the dimensions highlight issues that present insights into the emotions involved. Conclusions can be drawn that emphasize the multi-dimensional nature of meals and the service encounter, and complex influences on contemporary young people relative to culinary taste and consumption as expressed within home and commercial environments. Their relevance for hospitality business management is investigated.

Occasion

Table 10.1 summarizes the main categories of occasion selected, associated symbolism and indicates the numerical breakdown. Given the age group of the respondents it is hardly surprising that 18th and 21st birthdays dominate. This is followed by the 'kith and kin' motivation for hospitality where close and geographically distant family had the opportunity to bring the generations together to celebrate and mark special events. The next category illustrates the rewarding gift of hospitality by family members and close friends to celebrate achievement. For example, this took the form of completion of

Occasion	Symbolism	Number of respondents
Birthday	Coming of age	13
Family reunion	Kith and kin	12
Achievement	Rewarding gift	10
Holiday with friends	Childhood to adulthood	7
Holiday with family	Sharing the moment	6
Cultural/religious ceremony	Routines and rituals	6
Life course change	Demonstrate care	4
Staff night out	Politically driven	3
Romance	Communicate love	2
Total		63

Table 10.1 Most memorable meal occasions

outdoor endurance test, collecting the Duke of Edinburgh Award at Holyrood Palace, being accepted for university, and, rather paradoxically, winning a weight loss bet! The respondents who selected a meal while on holiday with friends did so in that it was symbolic because for most of them it was the first holiday without their parents. It let them 'be ourselves', representing a freedom from parental guidance, and marked a transition from childhood to adulthood. In contrast, the holiday with the family tended to be symbolic in that it was the last, or that it freed family members from the stresses of working life, providing the family with a rare occasion to sit round a meal table together sharing the moment.

The cultural/religious ceremony reflected a cultural diversity in focusing on celebrations associated with the Chinese New Year and Christmas in various European countries. This revealed the routines and rituals that guide and order such traditional events. The life course change occasion emphasize the respondents' stage in life which involved them in a gap year, or leaving home and friends to go to university. The staff night out represented a deliberate arrangement to move employees from a work to a social environment to facilitate their socialization within the organization. This indicates in the respondents a desire to establish a sense of belonging; a potentially politically driven motive. Finally, there is the occasion of romance where the meal is chosen as a means to communicate love.

Implicit in the self-selecting nature of the meal occasion, is exclusion of others. In addition, the characteristics of the sample means that dining experiences may be limited, with few respondents being in a position to have experienced anything other than family/friend meal events. Furthermore, few will have yet participated in business or professional meal events. Thus, it is perhaps not surprising that the majority of the respondents chose meal occasions that held symbolic emotional value associated with rites of passage and/or separation and reunion (Gillespie and Morrison, 2001). Often these were found in combination, where the celebration of a rite of passage was given an extra emotional *frisson* because it involved imminent separation from, or reunion with, family and close friends. Cullen (1994) suggests this may represent a response to prevalent social trends that tend to undermine communal meal occasions, thereby conferring value by their exception. It would appear that there is a dominant social expectation that life events are be marked in a way that includes some sort of communal meal occasion. This may well be a response to how the respondents think they should be seen to behave according to prevailing fashions, images and conventions (Finkelstein, 1989; Wood, 1994). Significance is defined and reinforced because of the celebratory nature and emotional charging of such occasions, and provides an insight to contemporary social values. For example:

> The reason that everyone was there, was to celebrate the marriage of two people, which in its own right made the day a very special day; or in today's society, many people will never know or experience fifty years spent with one person, so what better way to celebrate than with your family.

Thus, traditional and prevalent social trends and conventions influence social behaviours, and contribute to the intensity of the symbolic emotional value associated with the selected meal occasions. These factors appear to directly shape and enhance the overall experience, setting it apart from those of a less memorable nature.

Company

None of the respondents described a meal eaten alone. Only three referred to the involvement of two people and this tended to refer to encounters of a romantic or courtship nature. The majority described occasions involving relatively large numbers of people. The company element could be divided into core and peripheral. Primarily the core company was variously composed of family, close or longstanding friends, and ages that crossed generations. This provides evidence of the perpetuation a social reproduction of the family to reinforce a coherent ideology of it through social structures (Charles and Kerr, 1988; cited in Bell and Valentine, 1997, p. 62). Furthermore, the composition of the company served to signify who is family or close friend and who is unfamiliar or an outsider to the described social group. Where the members of the company were unfamiliar, it was acknowledged that by the end of the meal the sharing of hospitality had turned *'strangers into friends'* (Lashley, 2000). For example, relative to the category of 'staff night out' (Table 10.1), it allowed new members of staff to *'break the ice'* and forge better relations that fostered a sense of belonging and security. The peripheral company to the core was recognized as co-producer in the creation of the meal experience, and was identified as being composed of restaurant hosts, service staff and other customers including visiting celebrities.

It is apparent that a sense of security, social cohesiveness, belonging and trust derived from the established interpersonal relationships, particularly but not exclusively within the core company, contributed positively to the potential for each individual to enjoy the meal. A dominant finding was that the core company *'let me be myself'*, and *'did not put me under pressure'*. It allowed getting drunk in public, and disregard for spoiling the enjoyment of other restaurant customers through relaxed social behaviours, such as loud hilarity and singing. This indicates the existence of a 'social group comfort zone' that connects with a quest for the satisfaction of emotional needs. These appear to be perceived as more important than those of self-esteem and status derived from, for example, romantic/sexual encounters. This could be taken as a reflection of the changing attitudes and relationships between young people compared to those of earlier generations. An alternative interpretation may be that there has been a change in cultural values as contemporary young people draw self-esteem from traditional values of kinship and friendship as an antidote to challenges of living in the modern world (Elias, 1978). Thus, with so-called traditional family boundaries and emotional securities being eroded and replaced with increasing uncertainty, the symbolism of the communal/family meal occasion takes on heightened meaning. As suggested by Giddens (1990), it becomes valued as an object, employed as a means to re-embeded social cohesiveness and belonging in an increasingly fragmented and fragile social world. Thus, it attracts high cultural value as a means of stimulating social cohesion and reinforcing traditional values contributing to the construction of their social worlds. In many ways meals perform the community meeting point which Adelman et al. (1994) suggest are becoming an increasing feature of service in cities where many people live an individualized existence.

Atmosphere

Atmosphere is defined as the tone or mood conveyed by place, the attributes of which are influential as they interact with and influence the diners who subsequently contribute to the atmosphere themselves (Riley, 1994). Constituents may be the tangibles of interior décor and the intangibles of the meal occasion and service encounter, the interpretation of which will reflect the respondents' personal socialization experience. Constituents provide a holistic architecture to frame the place, which houses the expression of certain emotions and which is instrumental in their manufacture (Finkelstein, 1989). Consequences of a positive atmosphere were identified as a spirit of enjoyment between the members of the company that promoted a feeling of sharing, belonging and togetherness in a socially relaxed environment. In addition a sense of celebration and conviviality was conveyed through conversation, laughter, singing, dancing, and the sharing of jokes. Further unique features of atmosphere by category (see Table 10.1) included: romantic within 'romance'; sexual frisson within the company of the 'holiday with friends'; wanting to cherish the moment not present in the 'staff night out'; and a feeling of anticipation and excitement for the future within the 'life course change'.

A significant feature of atmosphere identified was a feeling of being 'at home'. This was experienced by all categories except the 'holiday with friends', as they were celebrating the very freedom from all connection with the concept of home. Connotations associated with atmosphere as warm, homely, cosy, traditional and friendly where highly valued, and contributed to the overarching desire for comfort and a sense perhaps of a knowable and non-threatening environment. However, it is of note that the circumstances that support these interpretations do not always superficially at least suggest these feelings, for example, décor is variously described as modern, exotic, fancy, prestigious, grand, splendid, stylish, magnificent, and elegant. While these adjectives are perhaps reflective on the special and memorable nature of the occasion, this is something of a conundrum in that they do not obviously seem to complement an atmosphere of 'being at home'. Furthermore, respondents could be reacting to a set of stereotypical signs (Johns and Howard, 1998) that are more varied in their accommodation of increasingly global mediated values, to reproduce a set of conventional cultural myths within the dining out repertoire. This demonstrates the power and widespread acceptance of symbolic signs to which consumers respond with a sense of genuine pleasure (Featherstone, 1991).

However, a more dominant dimension was identified as a contributor to atmosphere that influenced the emotions of the respondents. Value was placed on the qualities of those service encounters which facilitated the creation of a relaxed and comfortable environment. In this respect, those respondents who preferred to choose meal occasions hosted in the home provide insight. Their appreciation of the meal experience often stemmed from their perceived freedom from the restaurant environment and its rigid protocols, behavioural constraints and *'pompous waiters'*.

This may further support the proposal that for the meal occasions chosen in commercial premises the perceived emotional satisfaction experienced by respondents may stem from the replication of an 'at home' atmosphere. An 'at home' atmosphere has been achieved, and the service encounter managed in a way that overcomes atmosphere erosion through protocols and formalities. Certainly emphasis was placed on the familiar, fun relationships shared with service personnel, and on their enthusiastic attitudes. This in part may relate to the needs of younger diners, with the nature of the service encounter successfully reducing levels of self-consciousness and potential embarrassment (Goffman, 1969). Whether this approach to service was conscious or unconscious on the part of the service personnel is unclear. Nevertheless, it would appear to have contributed positively to promoting an atmosphere of relaxation and comfort within a commercial environment, perhaps indicating a means by which emotions are transformed into commodities for consumption (Finkelstein, 1989; Leidner, 1993; Wasserman et al., 2000).

Food

All respondents took for granted that the concept of the 'meal' constitutes an event with formal structured courses, that includes some element of hot food and some complexity of elements, rather than a snack. Few made comments on the value for money ratio, which may seem unusual given their presumably limited disposable income. Bourdieu (1984) provides a partial explanation to this finding in that it may be more important for the respondents to exhibit their cultural, rather than economic, capital in their display of good taste. Throughout the narratives, the position of food in the meal experience is subordinated to other dimensions, and this is common across both domestic and commercial environments. There are few examples of descriptions that go beyond basic level food knowledge, and they tend to imitate the character of menu descriptions or restaurant reviews, for example, *'Very nearly all of the food on the menu is one hundred percent fresh, local produce. Fresh seafood ranging from salmon caught by local fishermen, then smoked or pickled by the head chef, to prawns and lobster also caught locally. Fresh vegetables are cooked in such an original way they could be placed alongside those served in the Ritz'*. Where food does receive attention it is in relation to its ancillary functions such as: stimulating nostalgia for family, home and friendships; recalling links between individuals and points in time; and mediating across generations (Giddens, 1990).

The origins of the most dominant types of cuisine experienced by the respondents in their meals were Italian, Chinese and American. Cypriot and Swiss were experienced on holiday, Bulgarian and Danish by respondents of these countries of origin, African following the completion of charitable work, and camping food at the end of an outdoor endurance test. There was limited reference to food of British origin either in the home or in restaurants, and this was limited to those respondents who had been nostalgic for family and home while abroad, and those celebrating a traditional Christmas. This emphasis upon foreignness as attractive in food is not entirely unexpected (Randall, 1996; 1999). The respondents' choices reflect the cultural expectation that foreign foods are more desirable than British, and are regarded as more exotic, mystical and luxurious (Said, 1985). This represents a form of invented tradition or myth that underpins the conception of a memorable meal occasion for respondents, promoting the bourgeois ideology (Barthes, 1973).

Within the family reunion, cultural/religious ceremony, and life course change categories (see Table 10.1) there are instances of food being prepared by female family members in the home, particularly in families of Italian origin. These meal occasions were used to communicate a respect for family, and often involved traditional recipes, for example, '*brodetta di pesce, bistecca alla pizzaiola and zuppa inglese or totellin a l panna e prachuto* [sic] (*tortellini alla panna e prosciutto*)', which had been passed from one generation to the next which helped to reproduce embedded identities (Lupton, 1996). Others demonstrated the power of food to stimulate a string of nostalgic memories of love and belonging, such as from memories of a grandmother's cooking back in an immigrant's home country, or a reminder of home from something that a mother would traditionally make for Sunday dinner. This also may be taken to demonstrate an authentic expression of hospitality and reciprocity (Finkelstein, 1989), the symbolic importance of which is often signalled through the likes of table settings that employ the best of crockery, cutlery and glassware owned by the family member.

Dominant in the narratives was the recollection of over-indulgent consumption of food and drink and an evident belief that good meals can include food and drink not normally included in the diet due to concerns about body image, health and prohibitive cost. This suggests that the 'specialness' of the meal occasion can legitimize the temporary suspension of normal concerns and the hedonistic pursuit of pleasure (Bell, 1976). For example:

> The calorie count was high but I'd been starving myself all day for this meal, I intended to enjoy it, I usually don't drink any sort of alcohol when I am eating a meal as it puts me off the meal, but since this was a special occasion I felt I had to, and so I ordered one too many Vodkas and Cokes, but who was counting!

The apparent recognition of the unusual nature of such consumption may result from cultural conditioning which imposes excessive concern for body image and over forms of social conduct (Elias, 1978, 1982).

Setting

Specific types of settings included home, holiday home, restaurants, hotels, golf clubhouse, ferry, and mention of a private/ pseudo domestic room within commercial outlets was made in a few cases. The recall of meals in both domestic and commercial settings provides insights into the perceptions of authenticity and inauthenticity touched on by others (Asforth and Tomiuk, 2000; Warde and Martens, 1998). Though some find difficulty in seeing the relevance of domestic hospitality to commercial applications (Slattery, 2002; Purcell, 2002), others propose that it provides an insight into the nature of genuine hospitality which has obvious implications for managers in the hospitality industry (Lashley and Morrison, 2000; Morrison and O'Mahony, 2002; Scarpato, 2002). The respondents tend to support the view that the nature of hospitality is different in domestic and commercial settings. That said, a rounded understanding of the emotional impact of hospitality provision, despite the fact that the motives for provision are likely to differ depending on the setting, would be of benefit to those in industry.

The use of the domestic environment as a setting was most dominant in the categories of culture/religious ceremony, and life course change (see Table 10.1), where it was felt that the familiar nature meant that members of the company were freed from any rules about acceptable social behaviour that may restrict their enjoyment in a public, commercial setting. Warde and Martens (1998) explained this preference in that it conferred a special status on the guest being welcomed into the home, and the occasions had more chance of being relaxed, convivial, and informal than in restaurants as the host had greater control over the event. In contrast, dining in the commercial environment is seen to embody a degree of public display, however casual the occasion might be (Finkelstein, 1989). Comment was made of the social requirement to 'dress up', which contributes to the 'specialness' of socializing in a setting out with the home. This uncovers the diversity within the research sample, with some respondents enjoying the status and prestige associated with the participation in more formal ritualized events in public, while others prefer to engage in what they perceive to be more authentic emotional events in domestic environments. This reveals a complex interactive process between domestic and commercial settings. A common denominator is that both forms of meal occasion involve expressions of kinship and friendship (Bell and Valentine, 1997). Where the distinction lies is that an important function of commercial provision is the sale of commodified emotions of status and prestige (Finkelstein, 1989), through reproducing traditional protocols and formats ransacked from the domestic/family setting (De Vault, 1991; cited in Bell and Valentine, 1997).

A further aspect of setting identified refers to the scenic beauty associated with geographic settings and physical location. This is particularly emphasized in the holiday with friends and family categories (see Table 10.1) where the unfamiliarity of the location adds to the meal experience. It tends to involve what might be considered classically iconic romantic sites, such as: in view of the Manhattan skyline; beside the River Rhine; in an Italian Piazza; next to an illuminated swimming pool; and in sight of Edinburgh Castle. Aune (2002) refers to this as the conferment of 'enchantment', an aura of fantasy and feelings that enhance emotions and transcend the meal experience. Certainly, respondents indicated that the geographic and physical location of the setting directly improves the atmosphere and thus the meal experience. In addition, it would appear that in these cases, they experience an extra *frisson* of pleasure and excitement derived from the accumulation of social status and cultural capital that dining in such locations can bring, as noted by Finkelstein in her commentary on the fête spéciale (1989).

Service

The respondents are confident and articulate in their belief that much of the responsibility for constructing the atmosphere conducive to a successful meal resides with service personnel. In the home there is clear evidence of a gender division of labour with service performed predominately by female family members in a manner that is dedicated to ensuring the satisfaction and nurturing of all members of the company. While the gender division does not appear to translate to service in the commercial setting, the concept of guest satisfaction and nurturing perpetuates and appears to be more valued than technical aspects of service, such as silver service skills and menu knowledge. It is the 'soft skills', described as 'attentiveness', 'attention to detail', and 'desire to serve' that dominate. For example, *'The staff that evening were very attentive, although not suffocating, and seemed to have a genuine interest in helping the guests to enjoy their evening'*. This may indicate a contemporary informalization of rules of appropriate conduct traditionally associated with maintaining social order in public dining places (Warde and Martens, 1998). In particular, communication and interpersonal relationships figure strongly, such as: the genuineness of the welcome on arrival and guest/ name recognition; being made to feel special and 'at home'; personalized, friendly and interactive social connection during the meal; and an expression of appreciation of the custom prior to departure. The prioritization of these aspects appear to relate to the development of self-esteem and personal prestige, but the data also suggest that the respondents had experienced something akin to the authenticity of the welcome associated with domestic settings. For example, *'From the moment we entered the establishment we were treated wonderfully and the host of the restaurant was extremely hospitable'*.

Woven implicitly and explicitly throughout the narratives were chains of meanings that suggest a recognition that service in the provision of hospitality involves the management of emotions. In particular, was the emotional engagement of both guest and service staff in the quest for enjoyment and entertainment, and the need to make the guests feel at ease or 'at home' and special while still respecting their social space. Johns and Howard (1998) refer to this as the service attribute of 'emotional comfort'. Insightfully, there is specific reference made by one respondent to: *'the staff's successful emotional management of the customers'*. This concern for the emotional dimension of the service encounter may represent a key critical factor contributing to the success of meal occasions, yet there is limited systematic understanding in the field of hospitality management (Hochschild, 1983; Leidner; 1993; Asforth and Tomiuk, 2000; Lashley, 2001). This finding underlines the role of guest contact with employees as an integral part of the commercial product. Working in such an environment requires more than technical abilities. As Burns (1997) argues, this places an emphasis on 'soft skills', such as amiability, flexibility and tolerance that support high-touch service businesses. At root it requires emotional intelligence among frontline service staff and their management (Stein and Book, 2000).

Conclusions

Through the systematic analysis of the personal accounts of the young peoples' meal experiences and service encounters, the mythologies, values and meanings employed to construct their social worlds have been revealed. The findings are heavily context dependent on variables including: the symbolic significance of the occasion; socio-demographic profile of the respondents; and the degree of socialization and cultural conditioning inherent in the dining experience. It seems that the level of symbolic significance attached to the meal occasion influences the degree of emotional engagement of diners. It is this form of engagement and the resultant immersion in the experience which combine to confer status on the meal as a powerful cultural medium that transcends its obvious tangible value.

The choices of meal occasions may reflect the age and limited dining experience of these young people, in that it primarily draws on kinship and friendship groupings associated with rites of passage, life transitions, and family and friends separation or reunion. The use and reproduction of cultural mythologies surrounding the concepts of 'family' and 'home' are evident. Strong attachment to this ideology is demonstrated through the use of words, such as, 'cohesiveness', 'belonging', 'security', 'trust', 'tolerance' and 'emotional satisfaction'. The inherent expectations of social order, conformation to social conventions and norms, and stimulation of nostalgic associations and memories appear to be embraced to anchor and create their social worlds. This may be explained by prevalent social trends at work in an increasingly uncertain world that could be eroding family boundaries, communal eating patterns, and emotional securities.

Thus, the meal experience represents an event containing symbolic and emotional components, and it is multidimensional in nature. A dominant perspective presented was that when the event is produced in a domestic setting then the emotions associated with the meal, home and family will combine to offer a certain authenticity. On the contrary, production in a commercial setting is to transform a 'natural' commodity into one that is manufactured. Thus, emotions such as enjoyment, pleasure, enchantment, romance, sexual frisson, and excitement move from the spontaneous to the deliberately derived when in a restaurant setting. Furthermore, preconceptions of home and family are used as an authenticity baseline when comparing and contrasting domestic and commercial environments. Authenticity indicators include welcome and friendliness, security and freedom from threat, comfort and warmth, tradition and the familiar, privacy, and freedom from protocols. Commercial environments can be seen as unfamiliar, bound by rules and social expectations, requiring public displays of social status, and is described variously as 'exotic', 'prestigious', 'foreign', 'mystical', 'elegant' and 'grand'. These findings are important in that they represent a form of mental tool kit that these young people delve into to construct their interpretation of which hospitality experiences live up to their version of the authentic. Moreover, it emphasizes the symbiotic relationship between domestic and commercial environments and the manner in which knowledge of domestic hospitality can be used to the benefit of commercial management.

Specifically, it is proposed that in the quest for the most 'authentic' manufactured meal experience, commercial operators are best advised to get closer to consumer's mythologies to expose values, meanings and emotions of import from which new, lucrative market opportunities for service design and marketing activities may emerge. This is particularly salient to operators active in market segments that promote the special, emotionally charged meal experiences that are appropriate for kinship and friendship groups. Finally, the significance and role of the service encounter has been emphasized throughout this chapter. It places considerable weight on 'soft' over 'technical'

Hospitality, Leisure & Tourism Series

skills, and here again the qualities valued in the home and family can be employed to satisfy and nurture restaurant customers. This is particularly relevant to the youth market with limited dining experience. By creating environments which are characterized by their familiarity and informality, and in which your people can feel self-confident, restaurateurs can engage their customers in truly satisfying meal experiences.

Bibliography

Adelman, M., Ahavia, A. and Goodwin, C. (1994). Beyond smiling: social support and service quality. In *Service Quality: New Directions in Theory and Practices* (R. Rust and R. Oliver, Eds). London: Sage Publications.

Asforth, B. and Tomiuk, M. (2000). Emotional labour and authenticity: vies from service agents. In *Emotions in Organisations* (S. Fineman, Ed.). London: Sage Publications.

Aune, L. (2002). The use of enchantment in wine and dining. *International Journal of Contemporary Hospitality Management* **14** (1), 34–37.

Barthes, R. (1973). *Mythologies*. London: Paladin.

Barthes, R. (1977). *Image – Music – Text*. London: Fontana.

Beardsworth, A. and Keil, T. (1997). *Sociology on the Menu*. London: Routledge.

Bell, D. (1976). *The Cultural Contradictions of Capitalism*. London: Heinemann.

Bell, D. and Valentine, G. (1997). *Consuming Geographies*. London: Routledge.

Bourdieu, P. (1984). *Distinction, a Social Critique on the Judgment of Taste*. London: Routledge and Kegan Paul.

Burns, P. (1997). Hard-skills, soft-skills: undervaluing hospitality's service with a smile. *Progress in Tourism and Hospitality Research* **3**, 239–248.

Charles, N. and Kerr, M. (1986). The issues of responsibility and control in the feeding of families. In *Consuming Geographies* (D. Bell and G. Valentine, Eds 1997). London: Routledge.

Charles, N. and Kerr, M. (1988). *Women, Food and Families*. Manchester: Manchester University Press.

Cullen, P. (1994). Time, tastes and technology: the economic evolution of eating out. *British Food Journal* **96** (10), 4–9.

De Vault, M. (1991). *Feeding the Family: The Social Organization of Caring as Gendered Work*. Chicago: Chicago University Press.

Douglas, M. (1975). *Deciphering a Meal*. London: Routledge and Kegan Paul.

Elias, N. (1978). *The Civilizing Process Volume 1: The History of Manners*. Oxford: Basil Blackwell.

Elias, N. (1982). *The Civilizing Process Volume 2: State Formation and Civilisation*. Oxford: Basil Blackwell.

Featherstone, M. (1991). *Consumer Culture and Postmodernism*. London: Sage Publications.

Finkelstein, J. (1989). *Dining Out: A Sociology of Modern Manners*. Cambridge: Polity Press.

Giddens, A. (1990). *The Consequences of Modernity*. Cambridge: Polity Press.

Gillespie, C. and Morrison, A. (2001). Commercial hospitality consumption as a live marketing communication system. *International Journal of Contemporary Hospitality Management* **13** (4), 83–188.

Glaser, B. and Strauss, A. (1967). *The Discovery of Grounded Theory*. Chicago: Aldine Publishing Co.

Goffman, E. (1969). *The Presentation of Self in Everyday Life*. New York: Anchor Books.

Gofton, L. (1995). Dollar rich and time poor? Some problems in interpreting changing food habits. *British Food Journal* **97** (10), 11–16.

Gyimothy, S. (2000). Odysseys: analyzing service journeys from the customer's perspective. *Managing Service Quality* **10** (6), 389–396.

Hochschild, A. (1983). *The Managed Heart: Commercialisation of Human Feelings*. Berkley: University of California Press.

Johns, N. and Howard, A. (1998). Customer expectations versus perceptions of service performance in the foodservice industry. *International Journal of Service Industry Management* **9** (3), 248–265.

Lashley, C. (2000). *Hospitality Retail Management*. Oxford: Butterworth-Heinemann.

Lashley, C. (2001). *Empowerment: HR Strategies for Service Excellence*. Oxford: Butterworth-Heinemann.

Lashley, C. and Morrison, A. (2000). *In Search of Hospitality: Theoretical Concepts and Debates*. Oxford: Butterworth Heinemann.

Leidner, R. (1993). *Fast Food Fast Talk: Service Work and the Routinization of Everyday Life*. Berkely: University of California Press.

Lupton, D. (1996). *Food, the Body and the Self*. London: Sage Publications.

Mann, S. (2000). *Hiding What We Feel, Faking What We Don't*. Shaftesbury: Element.

Mitchell, J. (1999). The British main meal in the 1990s: has it changed its identity? *British Food Journal* **101** (11), 871–883.

Morrison, A. and O'Mahony, B. (2002). Hospitality: A Liberal Introduction. *Journal of Hospitality and Tourism Management* **9** (2), 189–197.

Purcell, C. (2002). Review of in search of hospitality, *International Journal of Hospitality Management*, **21** (2), 203–205.

Randall, S. (1996). *Television Representations of Food*. Unpublished MSc dissertation, Edinburgh: Queen Margaret University College.

Randall, S. (1999). Television representations of food: a case study. *International Journal of Hospitality and Tourism Research, The Surrey Quarterly* **1** (1), 41–54.

Riley, M. (1994). Marketing eating out. *British Food Journal* **96** (10), 15–18.

Saussure, F. de (1916/1974). *Course in General Linguistics*. London: Fontana.

Scarpato, R. (2002). Gastronomy studies in search of hospitality. *Journal of Hospitality and Tourism Management* **9** (2), 152–163.

Slattery, P. (2002). Finding the hospitality industry. *Journal of Hospitality, Leisure, Sport and Tourism Education* **1** (1).

Stein. S. and Brooks, H. (2000). *The EQ Edge: Emotional Intelligence and Your Success*. London: Kogan Page.

Storey, J. (1993). *An Introductory Guide to Cultural Theory and Popular Culture*. Hemstead: Harvester Wheatsheaf.

Warde, A. and Martens, L. (1998). Eating out and the commercialization of mental life. *British Food Journal* **100** (3), 147–153.

Wasserman, V., Rafaeli, A. and Kluger, A. (2000). Aesthetic symbols as emotional cues. In *Emotion in Organisations* (S. Fineman, Ed.). London: Sage Publications.

Wood, R. (1994). Dining out on sociological neglect. *British Food Journal* 96 **(10)**, 10–14.

Young, M. and Wilmott, P. (1975). *The Symmetrical Family*. Harmondsworth: Penguin.

Index